# The Formation of the
# Lutheran Church in America

JOHANNES KNUDSEN

# The Formation of the
# Lutheran Church in America

FORTRESS PRESS        PHILADELPHIA

COPYRIGHT © 1978 BY FORTRESS PRESS

Library of Congress Cataloging in Publication Data

Knudsen, Johannes, 1902–
    The formation of the Lutheran Church in America.

    1.  Lutheran Church in America.   I.   Title.
BX8048.2.K58      284'.133'09      77-15235
ISBN 0-8006-0517-9

6508K77    Printed in the United States of America    1-517

# Contents

# Foreword

Among the many efforts at church union in the mid-years of the present century were two that affected the eight Lutheran bodies that made up the National Lutheran Council. Four of the eight bodies united in 1960 to form the American Lutheran Church. The remaining four constituted the Lutheran Church in America in 1962. It is to tell the story of the latter church that this book has been written.

To indicate the scope of the preparation for union it would have been easy simply to list the many dates when the Joint Commission on Lutheran Unity (JCLU) and its numerous committees convened from 1956 to 1962, together with the subject matter of each meeting. But to understand fully the real significance of this effort of union dates, facts, and figures are not enough. There must also be a presentation of the varied ethnic, historical, and theological backgrounds of the four churches involved to allow for any grasp of the contribution of each of the four traditions to the church in process of formation. As well, there must be a careful study and deepened understanding of the common confessional position of the uniting churches which would brook no compromise of that confessional stance in the structure documents. Thus we can appreciate the intricate and arduous task undertaken by the JCLU in its negotiations for union.

But why publish the story of these union efforts almost twenty years after the fact? Certainly this is not for the purpose of "pulling up the roots" to see if there is any life there! Certainly it is not to find fault with the JCLU and its efforts at building a church, because from our present vantage point we may see more clearly what should have been done, or not done, some two decades ago! No, the purpose is to detail an important bit of American Lutheran church history at a given point in time for the information and enjoyment of present and future members of the church and of the interested public generally. To do this while participants in the work of the JCLU are still living is to give to the story a vitality which always comes from the testimony of living witnesses and workers.

The author who has undertaken the task of putting into readable form the record of the JCLU is admirably suited for the task. He served as the Assistant Secretary and Treasurer of the Commission for the entire six years of its activity. From that vantage point he could observe the pros and cons of debate and the give and take of argumentation. He is a highly competent church historian and a theologian of deep insight. He is a storyteller par excellence! The result of his work is a presentation that unfolds like a tale to be told. The language is precise, nontechnical, easily understood. There are evidences of the author's sly humor, which gives added life to what he is telling. He doesn't hesitate to express personal opinions different from those of the majority. In so doing he raises questions that need, even yet, to be thought through in order to enrich the ongoing life of the church initially brought into structured form through the Joint Commission on Lutheran Unity.

—MALVIN H. LUNDEEN

# Preface

The following account has grown out of the encouragement of friends and colleagues and out of a personal desire to tell a story. As an historian I know the risks of writing history before the facts have been adequately sifted and the prejudices of the situation have died down. On the other hand, I also know the need for contemporary narration and evaluation before the living memory of details fades away. I have therefore tried to write with the discipline of an historian, which is primarily that of being thorough and fair. But I have also tried to give a personal account of an enterprise of which I was a part, so that the facts and figures become more than records and statistics. I have allowed myself the privilege of opinion, hoping that I have not been unfair to persons but realizing that there is a real necessity for putting things in place.

The records of the Joint Commission on Lutheran Unity, including minutes, reports, appendixes, and exhibits, are on deposit in Chicago in the archives of the Lutheran Church in America. They have been used by permission of the LCA Archivist, James B. Crumley, Jr., and the Associate Archivist, Joel W. Lundeen. My special thanks go to Pastor Lundeen for his valuable assistance and guidance.

The story is now placed before the public in the hope that it may bring information, understanding, and even guidance. I dedicate it to the many committed people who took part in the work of the Joint Commission on Lutheran Unity as it laid the groundwork of our church.

# 1. Background

"1956 was the year in which the Lutherans of America stood up and were counted. Rails were laid that will run far into the future; their direction looks as if it is firmly set for a long time to come. New boundary lines were traced, criss-crossing in a deplorable and even sinful way over the broad Lutheran plains of this continent; substantial stone fences are being built on them, higher and higher. Years like 1956 are frequently the most decisive of all, far more so than the later dates when everything is consummated."

While the above statement from Franklin Clark Fry's *Desk Book* letter on "The State of the Church" (January 1957) reflects the disappointment that the Lutheran churches of America could not meet in a single merger but separated into two, with a large church on the sidelines, it nevertheless also reflects the ecumenical mood of the decade and the joy that mergers were taking place. Twenty-five years ago there was a mood for unification which is not easy to recapture today. This mood was partly one of penitence for war and disruption. Like so many other issues in the postwar era, church relations were viewed with a passion for wound-binding and soul-mending without regard to problems. There was a bending together of bodies that had been fractious, suspicious, and even hostile toward one another. In that mood, division was an overriding sin, contrary to biblical testimony and contemporary church ethics. The word "sinful" slips easily into Dr. Fry's discourse.

The penitential mood was perhaps superficial. Behind it, however, lay a generation-long reversal of post-Reformation trends toward fraction and isolation. The nineteenth century had witnessed an intense struggle on the part of the new Lutheran churches on the American continent for separate and independent identity, and the Protestant rivalry had been fierce. But in the abatement of pioneer self-assertion and in the discovery of wider communities, the trend had been reversed by post–World War I mergers. The

11

Norwegian churches had united in 1917 and the United Lutheran Church in America was formed in 1918. In that same year the National Lutheran Council came into being. The American Lutheran Church and the American Lutheran Conference were formed in 1930. Before the middle of the present century the movement toward unity had been capped by national and international dialogue and rapprochement culminating in organization of the Lutheran World Federation (1947), the World Council of Churches (1948), and the National Council of Churches (1950). Once wary and suspicious neighbors had been drawn into the friendly and non-contaminating frameworks of mutual efforts. Within the Lutheran family on this continent, the National Lutheran Council was especially effective in overcoming estrangement and in increasing the knowledge of one another through practical cooperation.

Other and more special factors were also at work toward union in the middle of the century. Most of the Lutheran churches with the ethnic background of nineteenth-century immigration had evolved through the routine patterns of ethnic sensitivity and language change. As church bodies began to cooperate with one another in many practical matters, church members looked at their neighbors and wondered why they lived in separate groups when their beliefs and practices had come from the same historic source. Practically speaking, the laity began to wonder whether the duplication of institutions and efforts was necessary. As mother tongues faded and as cultural gaps widened across the Atlantic, the supportive and sharing relationship with "mother churches" in Europe was gradually becoming less important and even practically difficult. For smaller church bodies, their continued independent existence in the face of rising institutional demands and the erosion of membership in the pervasiveness of Americanization and ecumenicity became a matter of survival, and this led to a desire for stronger indigenous Lutheran ties.

Out of this situation arose the Lutheran Church in America, and as the focus of inquiry is directed toward it in evaluation of its current stature twenty years after the merger, the mood of that era largely eludes us. The serenity of the fifties was shattered by the turbulence of the sixties. The anticipated blessings of comprehensive institutions have been obscured by the bane of bureaucracy. The fellowship of congregations has not flowered to the extent that was expected. The frictions of varying styles of church and individual living, particularly in the placement of pastors, have caused controversy and even anguish. The fiscal costs of wider efforts have risen sharply. Hopes of further mergers seem more distant, and fractions have again appeared on the pan-Lutheran scene. The enthusiasm and optimism which prevailed a generation ago seem unreal to many people today.

Yet the major benefits looked for in the merger that created the Lutheran Church in America remain and are largely unchallenged, although structural changes have been found to be necessary. In order to understand properly what the main characteristics, and even the benefits, were in comparison with what was, and in order to get a feeling for why things were done the way they were, a look at the process of merger may be useful, and the time seems to have arrived for such a look. The knowledge of what happened is lodged in the memory of men, mature then and now twenty years older, and some of the most knowledgeable of them are no longer among us. The recorded facts are there, in the minutes, in the reports, and in other documents, but they must be dug out and interpreted in order to present them in a summary and evaluative manner. It is hoped that this volume may serve that purpose and that the event and process of the merger might be a source of knowledge and understanding, perhaps even a guide.

The Lutheran Church in America came into being in 1962 as a joint continuation of four churches: the United Lutheran Church in America, the Augustana Evangelical Lutheran Church, the Finnish Evangelical Lutheran Church of America, and the American Evangelical Lutheran Church. Each brought separate and distinct features to the union, features that have roots in their history and common life. Their individual history shall not be told here; it is too long and comprehensive and it has adequately been chronicled by competent historians. A brief sketch seems in order, however, outlining the main features of the four churches and stressing the factors that were important for union, such as their propensity toward merger or their problems with merger, their polity or organization, the character of their church life, their predominant traditions, their experience—or lack of it—in mutual relations, and so on. The sketches will not follow a uniform pattern and should not be compared too rigidly, for the gifts which these several churches brought to the union—and the idiosyncrasies as well— were different, "peculiar" in the positive sense of that word. "Let every creature rise and bring / peculiar honors to our king."

The *United Lutheran Church in America* (ULCA) was characterized by several distinct factors, the main one being its long history in America. It was an American church to a greater extent than any other Lutheran church. Originally and through continued connections it had a German background, but its participation in American life predated even the history of our country as a nation. It had additional elements of tradition from immigrants other than German; on the whole, however, the ethnic transition was so distant that its ethnic origins were no longer a dominant factor. Geographically the ULCA was primarily a church of the east and the south. Its organization had followed immigrants across the continent, primarily where the English language was needed and required for the life of the church, and it was truly a national organization. The overwhelming concentration of membership was in the eastern area, with Pennsylvania as the motherland of the majority.

"The history of the Lutheran Church in America is a story of Synods, their formation, their divisions and mergers. It is also a story of attempts to relate Synods to one another in comprehensive organizations."* The nature and development of synods will be discussed in a later chapter; suffice it to say here that some of the synods that had sprung up in the east and the south were gathered into a General Synod in 1820. These synods were served by the seminary established at Gettysburg, Pennsylvania, in 1826. The General Council owed its origin to a confessional reaction against what was believed to be a prevalent spirit of doctrinal laxity in quarters of the General Synod. In particular, those synods that formed the General Council took strong exception to the "American Lutheranism" advocated by Samuel S. Schmucker. Synods belong-

* The Commission on Ecumenical Relations of the Augustana Church, reported in JCLU minutes, p. 8.

ing to the General Council were reinforced by a newer immigration in rather large numbers of German Lutherans who were strongly influenced by the confessional revivals of nineteenth-century Germany. The result was a secession and the formation of a separate body, the General Council, in 1867, which was centered around a new seminary at Philadelphia, founded in 1864. There were now two general bodies gathered around two seminaries, "one moderately conservative and 'American,' the other, strictly conservative and 'German.'"* During the Civil War the Lutheran churches of the South broke away from their northern relations to create a third body, the General Synod of the South (1862). As a matter of record, although not pertinent to this study, it should be noted that a large number of other church bodies, generally called synods, with ethnic and doctrinal emphases, were established on the American scene during the last two thirds of the nineteenth century.

The growth of the churches and of the nation in general from Civil War times to the end of World War I created many opportunities for dialogue and common effort. The three bodies mentioned above—the General Synod, the General Council, and the General Synod of the South—gradually moved toward each other again. They expressed their basic and historic affiliation with one another in such enterprises as the publication of the Common Service (1888), a Catechism (1899), a common hymnal (1917), and a book of ministerial acts (1918). Common efforts at social reform and other contacts continued, and prominent personalities exerted mutually respected leadership. As a result, the three churches joined in 1918 to form the United Lutheran Church in America. This church thus had a sensitive experience in separation and re-union plus extensive experience in matters of cooperation matched by no other Lutheran group in the country. Its history was mirrored in its leadership, where strong men, created by the exigencies of their challenges, had emerged as national and even international figures. It was also reflected in an immediate and rather strong desire for a limited but nevertheless active centralized organization and leadership. Running parallel and even counter to this

* E. Clifford Nelson, ed., *The Lutherans in North America* (Philadelphia: Fortress Press, 1975), p. 232.

was the historic synodical emphasis with a loyalty to regional and traditional values, especially in regard to the seminaries which were considered to be strongholds of the various synods, the pride of the people, and the symbols of security. In a sense, the ULCA resembled the late-medieval political organization in Europe with an empire strongly centralized in regard to basic issues but with powerful duchies and baronies of a regional and local nature.

The *Augustana Evangelical Lutheran Church* (Augustana) came to the merger with a relatively long record of adjustment to American church life and a greater experience in interchurch cooperation than any other Scandinavian-based group. Swedish immigrants, arriving in America in large numbers since the 1840s and founding churches mostly in the Middle West, had joined with other Scandinavian churches in the Synod of Northern Illinois as early as 1851, and the leaders of that synod were engaged in the establishment of an educational institution even before they concentrated upon a separate seminary. The Augustana church was founded in 1860 and continued its separate existence until the LCA merger in 1962. During that period of separate existence Augustana had a long history of relations with other churches. In 1870 it had joined the General Council, but "it had often felt less than at home"* and it withdrew from the Council immediately preceding the ULCA merger of 1918. In 1930 Augustana joined the American Lutheran Conference, an association of five Lutheran churches, formed to a large degree to counterbalance the alleged liberalism of the ULCA.

Throughout this American experience the members and pastors of the Augustana church had retained their strong loyalty to their Swedish heritage even though the language question had largely been resolved shortly after World War I. Most prominent in this heritage was an emphasis upon the ecclesiastical and confessional nature of the church. The formal character of church order and church worship, including a traditional emphasis upon the role of the pastor as leader, and the declared doctrines of the church in Lutheran confessional statements, particularly in the Augsburg Confession, were the main features from Augustana's very beginning. The name Augustana, from the Latin title of the Augsburg Confes-

* Ibid., p. 375.

sion of 1530, emphasizes this confessional stance. Combined with this, however, was a heritage of Swedish nineteenth-century revivalism, or Pietism. The expression of Pietism in Augustana was less ethically confining than in other forms of Scandinavian Pietism, but there was a strong emphasis upon individual piety and growth in sanctification. Parallel to similar efforts in Europe, the personal quality of the Augustana emphasis led to strong expressions of what the Germans call "inner mission," namely, the founding and support of charitable institutions. The Swedes were forerunners in the establishment of hospitals and homes for children and the aged. There was also a real concern for the problems of society, reaching back to the slavery issue prior to the Civil War.

Through cooperation in the National Lutheran Council since World War I days and through the joint efforts of the American Lutheran Conference, the Augustana church had gained considerable experience in interchurch matters and its inclination had long been one of cooperation. Some of its leaders had gained national stature, at least in Lutheran circles, and its pastors had been well educated. There was perhaps an element of theological inbreeding with only one seminary given to education and research, but this was largely offset by contacts with modern Swedish theology, especially the theology of Gustaf Aulen and Anders Nygren, and the ecumenical leadership of Archbishop Nathan Soderblom of Uppsala.

*Suomi Synod* (Suomi), the Finnish Evangelical Lutheran Church of America, had the shortest history in America of the Scandinavian churches. Although there had been immigration of Finnish workers to mining and logging communities as early as the Civil War, the main immigration came late in the nineteenth century and the Suomi Synod was organized in 1890. Its congregations were concentrated chiefly in northern Michigan, Wisconsin, and Minnesota, although the synod had congregations elsewhere on the North American continent.

Finnish people have a sturdy and resilient quality of character built through generations of struggle. Their homeland is a beautiful northern area of lakes and forests, but cultivation and even survival required hard work and vigilance. Politically and culturally their history has been one of resistance to foreign domination. In many ways Finnish culture was isolated—even the language is almost unique among European language groupings, and spiritual resources were drawn from within. The Christian faith and the Lutheran Reformation came from western Europe, but the roots of Finnish culture reach down to the profundities of the *Kalevala* legends.* Contemporary Finnish culture is brilliantly expressed in poetry, music, crafts, and architecture, and the Finnish national spirit engenders intense loyalty and an independent spirit forged in the harsh confrontations of history.

Within the given circumstances it was inevitable that Finnish Christianity should foster strong and controversial points of view. Revival movements contended for participation and support in the nineteenth century, although basic Lutheranism remained relatively unchallenged. Three revival movements, each differing from the others in expression and emphasis, grew out of the intense and profound assertions of individual spiritual life. When immigrants congregated in a new land where the state offered no cohesive religious framework, division was inevitable. Under Juho K. Nikander, however, the cohesiveness of Lutheranism and Finnish culture brought congregations together to found a church in 1890, which joined the merger movement some three generations later, wavering for a time between one and the other Lutheran merger. The language transition came to Suomi somewhat later than to other Scandinavian groups, but this was not a factor in the movement toward merger.

Suomi people, with their century-old tradition of asserting independence and individuality, probably had more obstacles to overcome in regard to merger than any other group. That they nevertheless were ready to cooperate, when they entered wholeheartedly into the negotiations with distinctive contributions, was evidence of a sound and positive evaluation of the mid-century situation in American church life. Like the rest of the participants in the merger, they were basically Lutheran and American.

The *American Evangelical Lutheran Church* (AELC), known from 1872 to 1952 as the Danish Lutheran Church, was ready for merger in ways differing from those of the other three churches. It

---

*Kalevala* is the great national epic of the Finnish people, kept alive in oral tradition for centuries and published in the nineteenth century. It is a treasure of folklore and mythology.

was searching for a recognition and a fellowship often denied it in the American Lutheran community. In some ways an isolationist group, living within its own treasured resources of Danish church and cultural tradition, it had also been isolated by conservative Lutheran groups who regarded its basic views and attitudes as un-Lutheran and even heretical. In his history of Lutheranism in America, Abdel Ross Wentz dismisses the Danish Lutheran Church with the brief statement that others had "separated from the Danish Lutheran Church in America because of its false doctrine," but in the 1955 revision he changed that statement to "alleged false doctrine."* Although a longtime and active member of the National Lutheran Council, this church was not invited to join the American Lutheran Conference in 1930 nor to join the American Lutheran Conference merger negotiations in the 1950s.

The Danes had founded a church in 1872 which embraced a constituency located largely in the prairie states. Growth was comparatively slow, due in part to absorption of the immigrants into other Scandinavian settlements and in part to a common Danish indifference toward institutional church life. Emphasis on institutional growth was overshadowed by concern for the freer movements of the spirit, exemplified by a forty-year concentration on folk schools patterned after the well-known movement in Denmark. A theological controversy led to schism in the 1890s, and the synod which became the AELC never became numerically large.

The inner character of this Danish group, even in the caricature of it by conservative critics, today facetiously but ungenerously expressed in the unfortunate term "Happy Danes," was shaped by centuries of Danish church life and culture but particularly by the views and leadership of the Danish churchman N. F. S. Grundtvig (1783–1872). Basic to the ideas of Grundtvig's that permeated the AELC is first of all the conviction that the source of Christian faith and life lies in the sacramental worship and the living proclamation by the historic and universal church of the resurrected Christ and is particularly expressed in the confession of faith at baptism. This view shunts to the sidelines the conservative Lutheran claim that the

* Abdel Ross Wentz, *A Basic History of Lutheranism in America* (Philadelphia: Fortress Press, 1955), pp. 187–88.

Bible is the only norm and source of Christian faith and life, but it does not eliminate reverence for Scripture as the sacred, inspired, and authoritative witness of the church.

A point of difference was the anti-Pietistic stance of the AELC. Influenced strongly by Irenaeus, Grundtvig stressed the creation of the world and the creation of man in the image of God as expressed in the first article of the creed. He rejected the notion that the Christian life is separate and removed from the secular life of the world. In this connection he stressed two points. The first point stresses that the Christian life is primarily a human life which participates in the newness of life with God but is nevertheless a full participant in the human community. The other point emphasizes that the Christian community must be indigenous to the cultural community in which it lives.

The readiness of the AELC for merger was stimulated by the attrition that besets a small church community in a growing and increasingly interrelated American society, religiously as well as culturally. An abortive attempt to joint the ULCA in 1955 prepared the ground for acceptance of the invitation to cooperate in 1956.

* * *

Following World War II the mid-century merger mood brought about tangible efforts to join Lutheran churches to one another. The first general move was an attempt to expand the National Lutheran Council into a federation, possibly as a first step toward ultimate merger. A Committee of Thirty-Four, representing the eight churches of the National Lutheran Council, was appointed and convened in January 1949. Several member bodies of the American Lutheran Conference were reluctant to join in a union with the ULCA, which they considered to be dangerously liberal, and therefore the effort came to naught. Instead, the members of the Conference moved, through its Joint Union Committee, toward organic union within the Conference. The cohesion of this movement failed when Augustana withdrew because it was "not open to all Lutheran general bodies and . . . did not include the consideration of the subject of ecumenical relations."* Augustana then joined with the

* Nelson, *The Lutherans in North America*, p. 505.

ULCA in extending an invitation to all Lutheran church bodies to participate in merger discussions. In 1955 the two churches invited all Lutherans to "consider such an organic union as will give real evidence of our unity in the faith, and to proceed to draft a constitution and devise organizational procedures to effect union."* This invitation was declined by the Lutheran Church/Missouri Synod and by the Joint Union Committee of the American Lutheran Conference, which rejected the idea of organic union of all Lutherans. The invitation was accepted by Suomi and by the AELC and with that the stage was set for the formation of the Lutheran Church in America.

* Ibid., p. 506.

# 2. Start

There was a subdued air of excitement on the twelfth day of December 1956 in the Conrad Hilton Hotel in Chicago, when forty-six representatives of four churches, gathered from many walks of life, met for the purpose of creating a new instrument to be called a church. A farmer from Nebraska, for instance, a businessman from Arizona, a lawyer from Philadelphia, a professor from Ohio, and a host of church officials, educators, and functional specialists sat down to organize, to work, and to become friends. There was no nervousness or anxiety to be noticed, only eagerness and anticipation, and a tone of friendly cooperation was set for a conglomerate that was to become a team which would meet many times during the next six years. In retrospect it must be said that the enterprise was harmonious and efficacious. There was never any personal dissension manifest and many of the participants formed close friendships which transcended synodical affiliation. Leadership was strong but membership was also strong and uncowed. The argonauts set out in good spirits upon a successful voyage.

One question had undoubtedly occurred to many a delegate: How do you go about organizing a church? For the thoughtful the immediate answer most certainly was that we do not create a church in the profoundest sense of the word. The church is created by the spirit of God; we can only accept it and participate in it. A second thought, however, must have been, What we are trying to accomplish is not the creation of the community of worshipers but the building of the supportive and enabling institution which also is called a church and which is fully human. With this understanding we could go ahead with a clear conscience. If we had been assigned the task of defining and structuring God's church on earth in our situation and according to our needs, most of us would have refused to be so pretentious as to undertake such a task. The holy, universal church is not structured by our needs, insights, and defenses, but the institutional church must clearly be a fruit of these. The old saying that all beginnings are difficult did not apply to this meeting. On the contrary, the commission quickly reached agreement about agreement. Franklin Clark Fry stated this in his inimitable way in his *Desk Book* letter:

The AELC-Augustana-Suomi-ULCA negotiations are unique among all the church union talks I have ever heard of in that we squared away with tough, substantial issues at our very first meeting. That is a testimony to the courage and good faith of the four churches involved. No sparring with the air for us! Polite introductions were quickly past. The skittish tentativeness usual to such occasions was not necessary. We believe that unity among us is the will of God, we trust each other's sincerity, we started cutting at once into the snarl of problems in our path.

First, as becometh Lutherans if not all saints, we turned a searching eye on our agreement in the faith. To nobody's surprise we discovered that we are all Lutherans and that the consensus among us is a thousand times greater than the minor divergences in terminology resulting from our varying antecedents. No one among us called for the elaboration of new confessional documents under any euphemistic name.

The upshot, to the gratification of all, was a chorus of Aye, unanimously stating:

"After hearing the reading and interpretation of the doctrinal statements of the four churches here represented, the Commission rejoices to note that we have among us sufficient ground of agreement in the common confession of our faith, as witnessed by the Lutheran confessions, to justify further procedure in seeking for a basis for the organic union of the churches, including the formulation of a proposed constitution for a united church having in it articles on doctrine and practical matters of organization."

The resolution of agreement was the key factor. After its adoption matters proceeded smoothly. As a matter of course a certain amount of preparatory work had been done by the leadership of the four churches. A committee was named to formulate rules of procedure and its proposals were adopted. A name was chosen, the Joint Commission on Lutheran Unity, hereafter called JCLU. A chairman, a vice-chairman, a secretary, and an assistant secretary-treasurer were elected, and it was decided that the members of the Commission should vote as individuals but that no action taken by the Joint Commission should be binding on any delegation unless a majority of its members, present and voting, favored the proposal.

Three committees were appointed: a Steering Committee, a Committee on Doctrine and Living Tradition, and a Committee on Patterns of Organization, the latter soon dividing into two subcommittees—a Committee on Geographical Boundaries and a Committee on Powers and Functions of the Proposed Church. Subsequently a large number of task-oriented committees were appointed, and rather than cluttering the text with their names and membership these are listed in the Appendix. Their work will be mentioned seriatim in the following chapters. In general it can be mentioned that the committees worked diligently and well, meeting their schedules and applying their talents to a great variety of tasks. A special word of praise must be recorded for the Commission's chairman, Malvin H. Lundeen, and the secretary, Carl C. Rasmussen, who fulfilled their assignments with exceptional competence.

The most important committee was undoubtedly the Steering Committee, to which each church appointed two members: the church president and a chosen counselor. This committee made decisions concerning procedures, selection of issues, preparation of agendas, determination of timing, and so on and made proposals to the Commission. Although it met in executive session, the Steering Committee's decisions were regularly and faithfully reported and there was never any suggestion of undue back-room manipulations. Only once, in the final selection of personnel to head boards and commissions, did the exclusiveness of the Steering Committee become a factor, but more about this later.

At the first meeting the Commission could agree about agreement and it could prepare for future work and planning. It could, of course, make no decisions about substantive issues as yet, but it did listen to two important papers as groundwork for further debate. "Possible Patterns of Organization" was read by Henry H. Bagger, and "The Lutheran Doctrine of the Church" was read by Conrad Bergendoff. Both these papers will be discussed later. The issues were thus placed before the Commission, but before discussing these it might be interesting and pertinent to take a look at the Commission's membership. At the first meeting most of the delegates had not assumed individual identity for the others. Faces were yet a vague blur not related to the names on the roster. A few personalities stood out, of course, but many a quiet individual of the first days emerged later as an incisive and knowledgeable expert. When an effort is made to portray the delegation as a whole this is done in retrospect with the afterknowledge of six years of fellowship and fifteen years of remembrance, perhaps with the failings of an aging memory.

Taken as a whole the ULCA delegation was the most competent, reflecting the greater resources of the larger church. There was an imposing array of functionaries, theologians, educators, and practical-minded professionals. The geographical representativeness of the Commission was evidenced by home addresses from all over the continent, including, of course, Canada. In some cases it was obvious that a person chosen for the Commission was picked from among peers in order to satisfy regional requirements. There were people on the list whose forebears had belonged to the tradition of the other three churches. When the time came to man the task forces, the ULCA was well equipped.

Augustana, with a relatively large constituency and a strong background of experience, was also able to muster a very competent complement, drawn mostly from among church officials and educators, theological and otherwise. Malvin H. Lundeen, who chaired the Commission, proved to be a skillful, competent, and sympathetic executive officer. Conrad Bergendoff was probably the person most respected for his wisdom; Oscar Benson sparked the efforts; and P. O. Bersell wore well the mantle of an emeritus. Suomi and the AELC relied heavily upon their elected official leadership, led by their presidents, Raymond W. Wargelin and Alfred Jensen respectively, and supplemented by theologians, educators, competent pastors, and representative lay people. In addition to the members of the Commission, the JCLU drew upon a number of knowledgeable members of all four churches with expert competence in many fields to fill out committees and to undertake special assignments. Special recognition should be given to Martin Carlson of Augustana and George F. Harkins of the ULCA as consultants to the Commission.

The voting situation demands attention, for this was where proportional representation was abandoned. Although the ULCA represented almost 80 percent of the constituency, it was given only a few more votes in the Commission than the other churches. The numbers were: ULCA, 13 delegates; Augustana, 13 delegates; Suomi, 10 delegates; and AELC, 12 delegates. A showdown of majority votes on an issue therefore meant that the three smaller churches could have outvoted the ULCA quite handily. Such situations rarely arose; votes were most often split across delegations. It is to the credit of the leadership and goodwill of the delegations that party situations were few and even then were not on major issues. On one important occasion, however, the ULCA—as it seemed to the rest of us—intentionally placed itself in a position where it could report that it had been voted down.

A special word must be said about the person and influence of Franklin Clark Fry, without a doubt the person in the Commission who carried the most weight. He came to the task of organizing a new church with more insight and experience than anyone else; his competence ranged from matters of doctrine to correct punctuation. In one exchange of remarks he upheld the correctness of a member who pronounced "nomenclature" with accent on the second syllable. On the whole he was good-natured about his expertise, and he enjoyed sharing the story of his passing to the other world and knocking at the door of heaven. When Saint Peter asked him what he had been doing on earth, he allegedly answered, "I have been writing constitutions." "Come right in," said Saint Peter, "We need a new one up here." As the story goes, Peter assigned to Fry the task of writing a constitution for heaven. As he reviewed the finished document, Peter said, "Franklin, what's this part about God being a vice-president?"

Fry was so dominant a figure by the weight of personality, experience, and position, a fact of which he was well aware, that he could have caused a counterproductive reaction had he thrown his weight around in too obvious a manner. In many instances he therefore chose the less noticeable role of backseat driver. At times he was in the forefront of the action to push through a point, particularly in matters of precision. But on many an important issue Fry would choose one of two other courses. The one course would be to use his influence in the Steering Committee which proposed the agenda.

The other course would be to let varying and even opposing points of view run their course of argumentation to the point where a quiet word of counsel could help find a good outcome.  A variance of this strategy would be to let time run on without pressing an issue for decision so that the problem was decided by the fact that the opportune moment had been bypassed.  It will be seen later how a crucial issue was settled in this manner.  Fry's strategy was not opposed or resented by the Commission members; in fact, it was respected and even admired.  It was honorable, albeit clever at times, and it was not hidden from the members.  Everyone knew what was going on and could take countermeasures if such were needed.  On many an occasion there was a silent but appreciative chuckle as a strategy unfolded itself.  Even those who were affected by his strategy seldom resented it.

*    *    *

A word about procedure and time schedule might be useful.  The new church was given shape in a series of plenary sessions and committee meetings spread over six years.  During the early and formative discussions a main source of direction and dynamic came from the Committee on Powers and Functions of the Proposed Church, sometimes confusingly and with a reversal of names called Functions and Powers in the reports.  It should not be mistaken for the Committee on Powers and Functions of the Executive Bodies.  Its guidelines were gradually channeled into a number of specific committees of which the Committee on Constitutions loomed large in the early years.

The time schedule of planning and decision is of interest because of its impact.  The Commission had been organized in December 1956.  The target date was set for a comprehensive report to the churches, and a first vote by church conventions was to be in 1960.  This meant that a final vote could be taken and that the merger could be consummated in 1962.  The years for these votes had to be in even numbered years, for the ULCA met in conventions only in those years.  The consequences of this schedule were that a constitution had to be readied by no later than the spring of 1960.  But the constitution had to be built on a great amount of concentrated committee work, and after the sessions of organizing and planning in December 1956 and March 1957, the Commission settled down to a two-year period of research, discussion, and planning. Plenary sessions were held for guidance in December 1957 and March and November 1958, but the main efforts of those years were concentrated in committees. In 1959 the Commission again put its primary effort into plenary sessions so that the structure could be assembled. Sessions were held in March, May, July, October, and December of that year. In February 1960 a report was readied for the churches and it was distributed during the spring. This report contained a proposed constitution and a proposed set of by-laws for the church, a proposed constitution for synods, and a proposed constitution for congregations. For legal purposes the report also included an official "Agreement of Consolidation."

When reports of ratification came back from all the churches assembled in convention, the Commission settled down for the final effort. It met in plenary session in November 1960 and gave assignments to committees to work out the further and consequential details. Plenary sessions were held in March and September 1961 and in January, March, and May 1962, when the final disposition of details took place. The merger and founding convention, which had long been prepared by committees, took place at Cobo Hall in Detroit, Michigan, June 25–July 1, 1962.

The 1960 approval of the constitution by the church conventions was the first of two successive convention votes required by the constitutions of the merging churches. Unless the churches and the Commission had chosen to start over again with a first vote in 1962, the basic structure and character of the new church was therefore determined by the 1960 vote. There was never any challenge or serious opposition to the relative finality of the 1960 decisions, and although it was known that there were many practical problems yet to be settled, it was generally believed that none of these was constitutional by nature. Almost without exception these matters were subject to pragmatic decision, but inasmuch as they were to be adopted by the constitutional convention a number of resolutions were prepared for this purpose. Among them were the important matters of nominations for office and positions in the new church.

The expenses of the JCLU were shared.  Each church paid the cost of its delegation to the plenary sessions, but it was decided from the beginning that the JCLU should pay the expenses of committee and research work.  These costs were allocated to the churches on a percentage basis.  At the start there was a naive underestimation of committee costs and the first appropriation totaled $1,000.  By the time the work was completed the treasurer had disbursed $190,340.21.

# 3. Confession of Faith

The matter of formulating a confessional statement in our day is facilitated by the fact that it has been done many times before, but it is also made more difficult by the same fact. Lutheran churches accept a varying number of documents and the significance that is attached to them also varies. With the exception of the Apostles' Creed, which came into being as a worship and sacramental creed, identifying the God to whom we relate in faith rather than defining the revelatory events, the creeds have been formulated in order to settle differences or disputes. On the basis of the argumentation of the fourth century, the Nicene Creed (A.D. 325) expanded the worship symbol into statements about the divinity, recorded, as was the custom, in liturgical and rhythmic phrases. The Augsburg Confession (A.D. 1530) took a stand on the controversies that had arisen during the Reformation. The Formula of Concord (A.D. 1577) settled differences of opinion concerning Christian faith and life that had divided Lutherans in the generation after Luther's death. The early creeds and the Augsburg Confession were included in the confessional statements of the four JCLU churches, but the Church of Denmark had never accepted the Formula of Concord. Now the problem was to determine how precisely these ancient creeds were to be considered by a church in the middle of the twentieth century.

Besides the general concern in Lutheran churches for the historic creeds of past ages, American Lutheran churches have been involved in a special problem. Due in part to the strong influence in America of religious movements which derived their guidance and teaching directly from the Bible, often given over to specific interpretations based on a literal but arbitrary reading of Scripture, and due also to the strong rivalry for membership among independent churches in a land of religious freedom, it has become prevalent for an American church body to express its stand on the nature and authority of the Bible. This is a feature of American living not historically necessary in other lands, and it has resulted in the peculiar practice that the introductory paragraph of a church's confessional statement has to be a declaration about "the Word of God," its authority and inspirational nature. Lutheran churches, given to emphasis on scriptural authority ever since the days of the Reformation, have been caught up in this practice, and inasmuch as suspicions of unsoundness have been attached to anything less than a declaration of the literal inerrancy of the whole Bible, there has been a yielding to the pressure of fundamentalism.

It was obvious from the start of the JCLU that the delegations were not of a mind to be bound by the conservative American practice, particularly not in regard to the pattern of making an introductory and isolated statement about the Bible. For the merger churches the term "Word of God" applied primarily to the person who was called "The Word" in John's gospel, Jesus Christ, and to the gospel proclamation of God's salvatory deed. To express the basic view of the faith and its confessions, including a delineation of the significance of the Bible, in such a manner that positive elements were made clear and given priority, was considered to be an important albeit delicate task. The JCLU therefore appointed a committee of four theologians, one from each church, to bring proposals to the Commission. This Committee on Doctrine and Living Tradition was facetiously called the "K" committee from the names of the four members, Taito Kantonen (ULCA), Walter Kukkonen (Suomi), Axel Kildegaard (AELC), and Karl Mattson (Augustana). That Johannes Knudsen (AELC) occasionally substituted for Kildegaard did not change the "K" rationale.

As mentioned above, the four churches of the JCLU had accepted one another in fellowship on the basis of their mutual acceptance of the ecumenical creeds and the Augsburg Confession. To this there were no strings attached and there were no preconditions about the wording of a confessional statement or the order of preference. The pressure was there, of course, from the conservative American tradition, and accusations of liberalism were certain to be voiced if there was a break with the practice of starting out with a statement of biblical authority. The JCLU did break with tradition, however, and it wrote a confessional article consistent with its basic views.

By doing this it set a precedent for American Lutheran churches. It is therefore of interest to know some of the reasons and motivations for their action, and it must be said that the Commission acted in harmony and with no dissenting voices.

There were a variety of reasons for not starting with a statement of biblical authority, and especially for not making this an affirmation of literal inerrancy. Most importantly, it was believed that primacy should be given to the church's faith in Christ and the proclamation of him as Lord. He, and primarily he, should be called the "Word of God." Any statement about the character and authority of Scripture should emerge from this commitment to Christ. There was, therefore, no need to include any comment on literal inerrancy. Furthermore, the four churches had long been given over to a sound practice of scholarly research in regard to the Bible. It is a sad commentary on the slow pace of American doctrinal development and on the fanatic grip of reactionary groups that it should be necessary to explain and justify a scholarly biblical approach in the middle of the twentieth century. The attitude of the JCLU churches was neither new nor radical; it had been dominant in most Lutheran circles for at least a century. The time had now come for someone to show the consistency of convictions. Like the Communist scare of the cold-war days, the fundamentalist view had prevailed through threats and coercion. Sanity somehow had to break through.

The problem was not solely one of fundamentalistic authoritarianism, however. It was also one of Lutheran sloganism. Even in our day Lutherans have been influenced by the slogans or battle cries of the sixteenth century. One of these was the defiant outcry against papal authoritarianism as expressed in *sola scriptura* (by Scripture alone). This slogan concentrated upon a refutation of the institutional autocracy of the Roman church, and rightly so, but it closed its eyes to the significance of the living tradition so wonderfully expressed by Irenaeus. By perpetuating this cry Lutherans had cut themselves off from an important dimension of the Christian life. Recent studies have made this amply clear even as they have demonstrated the values of tradition. So the time had also come for Lutherans to rid themselves of a four-hundred-year preoccupation with the sixteenth century. Among the four JCLU churches, the AELC had a century-old background which had emphasized the living proclamation and the faith-confession of the historic church, but all the churches had lived with the acceptance of wider authority.

Added to these considerations for casting the confessional statement in a different way was the influence of Augustana and Suomi pietism. Pietistic conservatism in regard to conformity with the secular world did not carry over to a dogmatic conservatism, and doctrinal assertions in regard to Scripture, or in regard to the interpretation of Scripture, were not as important as the personal appropriation of Scripture's message. Of greater importance than anything else was the living Christ and his witness in the New Testament. It was therefore entirely proper to this tradition that an expression of the living faith in Christ, the Word of God, should be given primacy in a declaration of the church.

The time was ripe for setting a new pattern or a new approach to doctrinal statements. That the confessional statement of the JCLU, and now of the LCA, does this very thing is the cherished and considered opinion of many. This was not done in haste or without discussion. The Committee on Doctrine and Living Tradition worked for many months and brought several preliminary proposals to the Commission before final agreement was reached. The "Confession of Faith" of the Constitution of the LCA, Article II, which is printed below, begins with the proclamation that Jesus Christ is the Lord of the church. It states the belief that the Holy Spirit creates and sustains the church through the gospel, and it holds that the gospel is the revelation of God's sovereign will and saving grace in Jesus Christ. This is important, for Jesus Christ is the Word, incarnate and resurrected.

In this light the confession then declares the importance of the Holy Scripture as the norm of faith and life, as the inspired record of God's redemptive act, and as the continuing voice of the gospel in the world today. This is a strong, positive, and adequate statement about Scripture which avoids the negative and defiant aspects of fundamentalism as well as of seventeenth-century orthodoxy. If a future demand for further merger should require that the church back away from this, the effect would be deplorable. In order further to undergird and strengthen this position, Section 7 was added to Article II.

Sections 4–6 of Article II (see below) explain the stand of the church in regard to the historic confessional articles of the church. The stand is positive but qualified, and the choice of words was carefully considered. The church accepts the three ecumenical creeds as "true declarations of the faith." It accepts the Augsburg Confession and the Small Catechism as "true witnesses to the gospel," and in a deliberate and important declaration of unity and fellowship it "*acknowledges as one with it in faith and doctrine all churches that likewise accept the teachings of these symbols.*" Finally, it accepts the other symbolic books as further valid interpretations of the confession of the church.

CONSTITUTION OF THE LUTHERAN CHURCH IN AMERICA
ARTICLE II
Confession of Faith

Section 1. This church confesses Jesus Christ as Lord of the Church. The Holy Spirit creates and sustains the Church through the Gospel and thereby unites believers with their Lord and with one another in the fellowship of faith.

Section 2. This church holds that the Gospel is the revelation of God's sovereign will and saving grace in Jesus Christ. In Him, the Word Incarnate, God imparts Himself to men.

Section 3. This church acknowledges the Holy Scriptures as the norm for the faith and life of the Church. The Holy Scriptures are the divinely inspired record of God's redemptive act in Christ, for which the Old Testament prepared the way and which the New Testament proclaims. In the continuation of this proclamation in the Church, God still speaks through the Holy Scriptures and realizes His redemptive purpose generation after generation.

Section 4. This church accepts the Apostles', the Nicene, and the Athanasian creeds as true declarations of the faith of the Church.

Section 5. This church accepts the Unaltered Augsburg Confession and Luther's Small Catechism as true witnesses to the Gospel, and acknowledges as one with it in faith and doctrine all churches that likewise accept the teachings of these symbols.

Section 6. This church accepts the other symbolical books of the evangelical Lutheran church, the Apology of the Augsburg Confession, the Smalcald Articles, Luther's Large Catechism, and the Formula of Concord as further and valid interpretations of the confessions of the Church.

Section 7. This church affirms that the Gospel transmitted by the Holy Scriptures, to which the creeds and confessions bear witness, is the true treasure of the Church, the substance of its proclamation, and the basis of its unity and continuity. The Holy Spirit uses the proclamation of the Gospel and the administration of the Sacraments to create and sustain Christian faith and fellowship. As this occurs, the Church fulfills its divine mission and purpose.

The doctrinal confession speaks about the content of the church's faith life, but what about the nature of the church itself as a fellowship and as an institution? Article VII of the Augsburg Confession states that the church is the assembly of saints in which the gospel is purely taught and the sacraments rightly administered. This is a reference to the holy, universal church in which membership is determined by the faith expressed in baptism, no more, no less. But what about the specific church, the institutional church, the one which is about to be established? How do we declare the nature of this church and what is it to be? The confessional statement confessed the faith and made it clear how we wish to be understood by others, but what about the constitutional nature of our church, not in the sense of a written, human constitution but in the sense of that which constitutes? Is the church merely an institution created by a fiat of an arbitrary group of people? Does it intend to be a part of the great body of Christians?

These questions and many more undoubtedly swirled through the minds of the JCLU delegates. They were perhaps not articulated but they were undoubtedly there. Who are we to constitute a church? By what authority do we do this, and what will this church be like? There was one answer which readily presented itself and which did give part of the answer. There was ancient evidence in the church and there was almost universal precedent on the American scene that the faith fellowship is primarily experienced in the congregation. This is where people meet for worship, where the Holy Spirit creates the fellowship, where the gospel is preached, and where the sacraments are administered. Although the four churches might give up their existence as separate churches, the many congregations will still be there and will form a constituent part of the new church. The delegates to the JCLU are not only representatives of institutional church bodies; they are delegates from congregations. Thus the congregational polity of much of Protestant American church life offered its solution.

Is the congregational polity enough, however, to constitute a church? Does it not lack an important dimension? The same Article VII of the Augsburg Confession states "that one holy church will be and remain forever." This brings the elements of universality and historicity into the picture. Our church is not a new creation nor is it isolated from others. It is a manifestation by our will of the church that has had being since the Day of Pentecost and that shall continue forever. History and tradition must not be denied or excluded, nor must the universal fellowship of all Christians. As far back as the third century Irenaeus had asked, "Ought we not to follow the rule of tradition which they [the apostles] handed down to those to whom they had committed the churches?" There was no doubt in the JCLU about the answer to this question. The ULCA had a long tradition and the AELC had an intense commitment to the continuity of the historic church. A committee was appointed to look into this and related questions, and they brought in a proposal which was adopted with a few changes of wording. Again new ground was broken on the American scene. The JCLU declared the church to be a fellowship of congregations, but it broadened out to the whole church on earth and it entered into the company of those who had gone before as well as those who were to come. Read the stirring words of Article IV of the LCA constitution:

Section 1. All power in the Church belongs to our Lord Jesus Christ, its head. All actions of this church are to be carried out under His rule and authority.

Section 2. The Church exists both as an inclusive fellowship and as local congregations gathered for worship and Christian service. Congregations find their fulfillment in the universal community of the Church, and the universal Church exists in and through congregations. This church, therefore, derives its character and powers both from the sanction and representation of its congregations and from its inherent nature as an expression of the broader fellowship of the faithful. In length, it acknowledges itself to be in the historic continuity of the communion of saints; in breadth, it expresses the fellowship of believers and congregations in this our day.

The functional aspects of the new church were easier to come by and they were spelled out with the expertise of insight and experience. Article V of the LCA constitution is devoted to what is called "Objects and Powers." After a general introductory statement that "this church lives to be the instrument of the Holy Spirit in obedience to the commission of its Lord," Section 1 lists six stated objects. These functions breathe a loyalty to the church's basic task of proclaiming the gospel through Word and Sacrament and gathering and nurturing those who respond. They also demonstrate a breadth of spirit and experience when they affirm the unity of the faith and state that the church must give expression to that unity. The church must safeguard the pure preaching and the right administration of the sacraments by its ministers. It must strive for the unity of all Lutherans and it must participate in ecumenical activities.

Section 2 spells out the specifics of how this is to be done, beginning with the establishment and reception of congregations and the promotion of missions. The list includes such things as the education and discipline of pastors, provision for higher education, social statements, publications, worship guidance and promotion, adjudication of differences, delegation of work to synods, establishing of executives, managing a budget, and entering into relations with other Lutheran church bodies. The list is rather complete and comprehensive. It gives evidence of insight and experience, and it provides guidelines for activities in a good and proper manner. The list might, of course, have been condensed into more general rubrics of a wider nature, but it does not offend by its length and coverage.

If the responsibility of constituting a church with its basic theological assumptions and its many practical aspects weighed heavily upon the minds of the Commission members, the Commission took its time putting its motives and authority into words. The preamble was written as a final phase of the work on the constitution. Like a professor who writes an introduction to a book, explaining what he intends to do, after he has finished his manuscript, the Commission waited with this main introduction. Then it turned the task over to

Conrad Bergendoff, who was trusted to say the right things; he came up with a beautiful and profound statement. He was nudged here and there by Franklin Clark Fry so as to conform with the right preamble technique, which is supposed to include everything in one main clause without becoming burdensome or complicated. The preamble included that which had gone before, that which had been accomplished, and the promise of that which was to come. It could well serve as a model for the next merger document.

### The Preamble

In the name of the Father and of the Son and of the Holy Ghost. Amen.

Remembering the prayer of our Lord Jesus Christ that His disciples might be one as He and the Father are one, and believing that His Spirit is ever leading His people toward unity in the household of God, we of the American Evangelical Lutheran Church, the Augustana Evangelical Lutheran Church, The Finnish Evangelical Lutheran Church of America, and The United Lutheran Church in America, persuaded that the time has come when His unifying power should be manifested through a united profession of faith by these churches and through forms of fellowship which will make for a more effective stewardship of His gifts to us, adopt this constitution to govern our common life in Him and our united witness to Him, praying that He who is the Lord of the Church may thereby lead us toward a more inclusive union of all Lutherans on this continent.

# 4. The Structure of Synods

Two sentences from Franklin Clark Fry's *Desk Book* letter on "The State of the Church" (June 1958) set the stage for this chapter. The letter was written to his ULCA constituency eighteen months after the start of the JCLU and it expresses a general joy over and a satisfaction with the progress that was being made. The two sentences are:

> Even a quick reading of the JCLU proposals shows that a *new church structure* is to come into being.

> The new church will be more *church* and less *federation* than what we [the ULCA] have been used to over the past forty years.

The structure was less new to the other three churches, albeit more vast and complex than what they had previously experienced, for they had never thought of the church as a federation and could not conceive of it as such. Fry had made a comment about this in his January 1957 letter when he paraphrased the "Augustana men" as saying, "We want a church—not a loose federation of synods." The decision in regard to basic structure was therefore important, and to some extent sensitive, and behind the decision lies a tale of interest and significance.

Two basic premises for decisions on the new structure were apparent and unanimously accepted from the start. The one was that there should be a "general body," as it was expressed in the cautious terminology of the early discussions. The other was that there were congregations, already in existence, which were constituent entities of the church. The latter was expressed in a resolution adopted by the Commission at the March 1957 session, the first sentence of which reads: "A basic premise regarding congregations is that they shall be congregations of the general body and of a constituent unit."

But what about "intermediate bodies"? Were there to be such,

and what role were they to play? About this there was no immediate consensus; in fact, there was a great difference of opinion. All
four churches had intermediate bodies. The ULCA came to the
merger with thirty-two such bodies called synods. Augustana had
thirteen and called them conferences. Suomi had seven and also
called them conferences, while the AELC had eleven, which were
called districts. In the case of the latter three churches the conferences or districts were geographical and administrative units with
powers of administration and supervision delegated to them by the
church. The commissioners to the JCLU from these churches were
therefore predisposed to building a similar polity into the structure
of the new church.

In the ULCA the situation was both different and at variance. Its
synods, which were associations of congregations, had a long history
of significant and independent function prior to the formation of a
national church in 1918. They represented a principle of organization that placed the emphasis upon regional authority, traditionally
representative of values and points of view, and they regarded centralization as an authority delegated by the synods. This was a
federation polity with roots deeply embedded in traditional, doctrinal, and ethnic values, but it also had roots in the soil of American
political history. It might also be called a decentralized polity,
although it must not be assumed that all notions about decentraliza-
tion are to be equated with a polity of federation.

The synodical emphasis goes back to the early history of Lutheranism in America. While the first "mutual association" of Lutherans
in Pennsylvania was called a "ministerium," the term "synod" came
into common use in the middle of the eighteenth century. The term
means a "council," and there are suggestions that its usage had
Presbyterian origins. There is also evidence that it had a background
usage in Germany and that Henry M. Muhlenberg was urged by
the University of Halle to form a "synodical body" in North America.
Whatever its origin, however, the common, consistent, and early use
of the term indicated that it designated an association of congregations and ministers. Synods thus formed were jealous of their rights
and independence. When the population thrust across the moun-
tains into the Ohio valley occasioned the formation of new synods,

these were willing to cooperate with one another but they were not anxious to submit to the dominant authority of a consolidating agency. The General Synod was formed in 1820 and it became "a common agent in cooperative and interdenominational activities," but "the synods refused to delegate their traditional control of their own clergy and worship to the General Synod."* The General Council was formed in 1867, but its authority was limited to advice and arbitration in critical matters between synods. The ULCA, constituted by the joining of three church bodies in 1918, assumed more centralized authority. It had a president and an executive board, but it was careful to state in its constitution that the congregations are the primary bodies through which power committed by Christ to the church is normally exercised (Article III, Section 3) and that (Section 2): "The United Lutheran Church in America at its organization shall consist of the congregations that compose the Evangelical Lutheran Synods which have been in connection with [The General Synod, The General Council, and The United Synod of the South]."

When the JCLU assembled in 1956 its delegates thus represented varying views in regard to the relation of the general body and the intermediate bodies. In general the three small churches were in favor of a unistructured church, as this was the pattern they knew. This consensus within these three churches harbored a variety of opinions, however. There was considerable inclination toward a decentralized organization, and this reflected not only a natural desire for diversity and regional fellowship but even a "populist" resistance to the dominance of the East. But very little sentiment, if any, in these three delegations favored a "federation polity," in which the synods were the constituent entities of the church, although the term "constituent units" appears in early documents.

The predominant sentiment in the ULCA delegations eludes the historian. It was known that there were varying and even opposing concepts, but the interior dialogue was not immediately known to the public. The varying views were expressed in a scholarly paper entitled "Possible Patterns of Organization" read to the opening

* E. Clifford Nelson, ed., *The Lutherans in North America* (Philadelphia: Fortress Press, 1975), p. 120.

session by Henry H. Bagger. He posited three possible avenues to structure, labeling them "extreme emphases" and suggesting as a matter of course that they could be modified or combined in compromise. The three "extreme emphases" were:

1. The congregation as the basic unit
2. The synods as the central units
3. The general body as the central and controlling authority

Bagger suggested that the Commission should "think of something somewhat more mixed in character" and added: "We shall probably do well to stick to a fairly conservative polity with an eye to the wider organizational merger possibilities of the future. A relatively loose organization may well be advisable at the beginning so that the parts may grow gracefully and peacefully together into what we want to do and become—with due allowance for diversity for the individual parts while cultivating the hearty union of all in increasing measure." He advocated that the Commission posit "at an early date the degree of centralization or distribution of authority to be sought . . . ," and he suggested that "mere federation or a conferential relationship is not enough since merger or organic union is both our directive and our aim."

Conrad Bergendoff read a paper entitled "The Lutheran Doctrine of the Church." Its substance is found in expanded form in his book *The Doctrine of the Church in American Lutheranism.** Information from the paper and the book have been used in the background story of the synods given above.

There were thus varying and even opposing views in regard to "intermediate bodies" when the JCLU settled down to create the structure of the church. What happened in the dialogue can best be traced through an account of reports and plenary decisions. A proposal at the first session of the Commission, December 13, 1956, to appoint a Committee on Patterns of Organization was referred to the Steering Committee. This committee, meeting in the afternoon of the same day, adopted a resolution that the Committee on Patterns of Organization should function as two subcommittees, ¿

* (Philadelphia: Muhlenberg Press, 1956).

Committee on Geographical Boundaries and a Committee on Powers and Functions of the Constituent Units of the Proposed Church.

The Committee on Powers and Functions thus became the first committee to wrestle with the problem of structure. It made many specific and important recommendations, some of which had implications for the function of intermediate bodies, but it did not make direct proposals about the organization of synods. At its second meeting, February 15, 1957, it considered a proposal that "the constituent units of the new church shall be charged by its constitution with primary responsibility in the matters of recruiting, beneficiary education, ordination and discipline of ministers, and shall be recognized as acting for the church as a whole in discharging these responsibilities." On June 29, 1957, it made a number of recommendations concerning a variety of items, many of which were referred to the "general body," such as publications, social action, and so on. The important statement about congregations also came out of this meeting. In regard to the sensitive issue of higher education, the committee recommended that "the general church body shall have a Joint Board of Higher Education which shall function through three constituent Boards." For theological education it proposed that "ownership and primary responsibility for administration and control of theological education shall be vested in the constituent units of the united church" but that "the General body shall have a major board or division of a board, with the power to: a. Construct a master plan of location of theological seminaries, b. Approve the establishment and relocation of seminaries within the church," plus six other items. The tenor of these proposals was thus to delegate authority to the synods.

The committee proposals, with their implications for the function of synods, were presented to the plenary session of the JCLU on September 18, 1957. After some discussion much of the report was referred back to the committee for further study and no decisions were made at the time. At the same plenary session, on September 20, a motion was adopted to create a Drafting Committee. This committee was activated at the plenary session on December 12 by a motion to appoint five committee members, one from each church plus the chairman of the JCLU, but there is no evidence from the documents how this committee functioned. Apparently it was replaced at the March 21, 1958, plenary session when the Commission adopted a recommendation of the Steering Committee that "upon nominations by the presidents of the churches a constitution committee be appointed, consisting of two members from the Augustana Lutheran Church, two from ULCA, and one from each of the other two churches, said committee to a) prepare an outline of a proposed constitution, and b) outline by-laws and/or standing resolutions." From then on the Committee on Constitutions became the most important polity-determining body and the Committee on Powers and Functions leaves the picture. In November 1958 it outlined its approach and method by reporting to the Commission on "A Definition of Task, A Statement of Basic Principles and Other Practical Matters" but not as yet on any substantive issue. The committee consisted of Franklin Clark Fry, chairman, and James F. Henninger for the ULCA, P. O. Bersell and S. T. Andersen for Augustana, Bernhard Hillela for Suomi, and Alfred Jensen for the AELC.

This important and hardworking committee, the Committee on Constitutions, appointed, as mentioned, in March 1958, made its first substantive report to the plenary session in March 1959. At that time it presented the Commission with a completely drawn constitution. Many details of this draft were subsequently amended, but the format and main content of the final product was established in this model. That much work had gone into the effort is evidenced by the fact that the constitutional proposal given to the Commission in March 1959 is marked "Fourth Draft."* The fifth draft was presented in May 1959 and included a complete set of by-laws. The committee produced in all about a dozen successive drafts of the constitution as time and debate went on until the merger in 1962.

In the draft of the constitution presented in March 1959 the matter of intermediate bodies was virtually settled. Article VIII, Section 1 stated: "This church shall be divided into synods, their number and boundaries to be determined by the church." Section 7 provided that: "The principal function of synods shall be shepherd-

---

* No copy of a first draft is available now, but the archives have produced a "Second Draft."

ing of their constituent congregations and ministers. . . . The synods shall have primary responsibility for the recruiting, preparation and ordination of ministers, for the reception of congregations and for the discipline of both ministers and congregations. . . ." The wording of the article was changed before the final adoption, but the decision in regard to the basic problem was clear and remained unchanged. The new church was not to be a federation of synods; the authority and function of the intermediate bodies was delegated.

Through the currently available documents it is not possible to penetrate the debate that occurred in the committee or behind the scenes to see how this part of the basic structure of the emerging church was determined. Should documentation eventually become available through personal papers or memoirs not now in the archives, the sifting and evaluation of evidence would require a more lengthy consideration than can be made now. One matter of concern, indirectly but vitally involved in the synodical debate of 1958–59, can be documented, however, from other JCLU sources. It concerns the matter of the ownership and control of seminaries, which will be pursued in greater detail in the chapter on seminaries. In this matter two concepts clashed. The one, primarily sponsored by Augustana, was that the seminaries should be owned and operated by the national body. The other, sponsored by strong elements within the ULCA, was that such ownership and control should reside in the synods. The conflict was hard and even bitter, as will be documented, but in this regard the synodical preference had already won by a narrow margin in the Committee on Powers and Functions, where it first came up. The decision there influenced the constitutional draft, and the proposed constitution of March 1958 stated that the synods should have "responsibility for ownership and administration of the theological seminaries of the church . . ." (Article VIII, Section 7, b). In the case of the seminaries the authority delegated to the synods at an early stage was substantial.

For comparison with the proposals of 1959 the current constitution of the LCA, as amended by every biennial convention since the merger, states in regard to synods in Article VIII, Section 7: "The function of synods shall be oversight and advancement of the mission of the church within their bounds by propagating the Gospel, conserving unity in the true faith and guarding against any departure therefrom, and encouraging the fuller employment of resources of spirit and means for the furtherance of the Kingdom of God." The synodical functions are spelled out specifically in Section 8 in four parts, each of which has three to six subparts:

a. Care of congregations.
b. Counseling and enabling of professional workers.
c. Planning, development and supervision of special congregational, institutional and special action ministries.
d. Interpretation and support of the continent-wide and worldwide work of the church.

The matter of determining the number and boundaries of the synods was the fascinating but difficult task of the Committee on Geographical Boundaries. This committee worked long and very hard and it produced a series of proposals, but a report on the nature and disposition of these would carry beyond the limitations of this presentation. Suffice it to say that the early impulse was to make the synods effective by as small a number as possible. Extensive studies were made of tradition and background, of loyalties and fellowships, of church statistics and national statistics, of economic surveys, of means of transportation and communications, of population projections, and so on. In the end the number and location of the synods that currently comprise the LCA were determined by vote and consensus in the Commission, and while there was an awareness of awkwardness in specific instances, there was a common feeling that the result was as well-founded, considerate, and practical as could be expected.

# 5. Central Administration

The fact that this chapter, which discusses the central administration of the new church, is preceded by the chapter on synods, is due to an arbitrary decision which carries no significance. The order of the chapters could well be reversed. It seemed practical, however, to dispose of the broad aspects of organization before turning to the concentration of institutional authority. There was also an inherent drama in the determination of the character and authority of the intermediate bodies which demanded prior attention, namely, the question whether they were to have inherent power or delegated authority. If the authority was to be delegated, then by whom—by the congregations or by the general body? The consequences of the decisions in this case were rather far-reaching, especially in regard to the ministry and the education for ministry, but also for the function of congregations, as shall be seen.

There was also an inherent drama in the decisions regarding the central administration, but an outside historian, reading the minutes and the reports, would have difficulty detecting this from their bare-bones approach. A church historian would know, of course, that points of view in regard to central authority have deep roots in history, reflecting the varying polities of churches. Although an extensive account of these points of view with their origins would occupy too much space in this presentation, it must be said that the Lutheran tradition is in continuation of the ancient practice structured into the Roman Catholic hierarchy, namely, that one person had a supervisory and authoritarian role in the relationship of congregations. The office of this person, while called "presider" in Justin Martyr's second-century account of the Eucharist, is strongly episcopal in the early church, and the superintendent of congregations is early called "bishop." After the Reformation, Lutheran churches in the political entities of central and northern Europe, which were ruled more or less absolutely by individual persons, chose to continue the episcopal leadership. This was in contrast to the Calvinistic practice which broke with the episcopal rule and adopted a "presbyterian" or "council" authority, a practice which also had roots in the ancient church. Most post-Reformation Lutheran churches were politically defined and came under the authority and rule of the "prince" to whom the bishop was responsible. Some churches narrowed the scope of the episcopal office more than others, and some even rebelled for a time against the title of "bishop," but the office generally prevailed.

Immigrant churches from Lutheran lands brought the precedent of one-person leadership with them to America, even though there was some resentment against the image of such leadership in the homeland. In at least one known case, among the Danes, the organizing convention specifically resolved *not* to provide for a bishop. It divided its central office into two, electing a presiding administrator and a separate "ordainer." Interestingly enough the "ordainer" was given an authority denied the president; he was elected for life, an episcopal prerogative. Most American churches, however, if not all, elected a president and imposed a time limit upon his office, spurning the episcopal title, perhaps under the influence of American politics and general organizational practice.

In the Joint Commission on Lutheran Unity there was no doubt or difference of opinion in regard to the central leadership of one person, and therefore there was no discussion of this. The new church, like its four predecessor churches, was to have one person as its head. Whatever debate there was concerned his title and his authority. Even in regard to these matters the documents offer little excitement, and we must turn to other sources to sense what was going on. Dr. Fry, for instance, illuminates the situation in his *Desk Book* letters, and after reporting the bare bones of the documents Dr. Fry's remarks shall lend some color.

Concern for the executive branch of the church was first expressed in the appointment of a "Committee on Powers and Functions of Officers and an Executive Body of the United Church." The committee consisted of C. W. Sorensen (chairman), Ernest D. Nielsen (secretary), Henry H. Bagger, and Douglas Ollila. It met on May 26 and July 22, 1957, reporting to the Commission on September 19.

The committee proposed that the officers of the church should be four: a president, a vice-president and budget director, a secretary, and a controller.  The president and the secretary were to be ministers, and the vice-president, who was not automatically in succession for the presidency, might be either a minister or a layman.  In regard to the president's "cabinet" the committee proposed a body named "executive council," consisting of the officers of the church; members-at-large elected by the church, consisting of ministers and laymen to a suggested number of twelve; and members of boards and auxiliaries.  The committee also suggested a number of items of administration for the council in regard to the common church work.  The Commission meeting in September gave tentative consideration to the report, but it struck out the idea of a vice-president who was also to be budget director, and it substituted the term "treasurer" for "controller."  It added the statement that the president should be "the executive officer of the church."

The committee met again on November 1 and worked further with the concept of officers.  It suggested that the "general church council" should have thirty members, equally divided between ministers and laymen.  In a subsequent meeting the Commission considered these suggestions and added that the president "shall be the church's leader and counselor in matters spiritual and temporal."  The give and take between committee and Commission continued through several meetings until the whole matter was taken over by the Committee on Constitutions, which incorporated and adopted suggestions of both committee and Commission.  In its first draft of a constitution, presented to the Commission (its own fourth draft) on March 1959, it proposed the wording in regard to the office of the president which carried through verbatim in all succeeding debate until the adoption of the constitution at Cobo Hall in 1962.

The president of the church shall be its leader and counselor in matters spiritual and temporal.  He shall be the executive officer of the church and shall preside at its conventions.  He shall see to it that the constitution is observed and that the enactments and policies of the church are carried out [etc.] [Article IV, Section 4].

The Committee on Constitutions also formulated permanent ideas for the Executive Council, namely, that it should consist of the three officers of the church together with fifteen ministerial and fifteen lay members. Its recommendations for the duties and functions of the council also prevailed through the final draft adopted by the constitutional convention (Article XII, Section 3).

In regard to the title of the executive officer, the Committee on Nomenclature proposed in a committee-meeting report dated November 19, 1957, that the choice be between "president-bishop" and "archbishop." This was considered by the Commission on December 12, 1957, and the minutes read: "Motion was adopted that 'President' be used as the designation of the administrative head of the merged church." Now for Dr. Fry's comments.

> The liveliest flurry occurred when a subcommittee came out boldly in favor of designating the chief executive of the new church as "president-bishop" or "archbishop" and its constituent units "dioceses" each with a "bishop" of its own. That got short shrift exactly as you would expect! Nobody, or practically nobody, agreed with the committee's "earnest opinion . . . that the use of the ancient and historic title for functions and leadership in the church will most effectively communicate (their) nature to the world-at-large and will command a respect that is most desirable" whereas strictly secular or business titles attached to ecclesiastical functions cannot carry such weight and have not done so in our Protestant practice.

> In the authentic American, or more accurately American Lutheran spirit, the commission did not take two minutes to vote this unpopular proposal down with will, almost with a shout. No doubt about it, that is the overwhelming and deeply ingrained sentiment of all our four churches! It might be disquieting, and some day it will be healthy, to do a little probing inside: to discover why we are so full of negative dogmatism on this point; why we so conspicuously do not treat it as the adiaphoron we profess it to be. . . .

> President it is going to be, and secretary and treasurer, executive council and boards, synods and districts. The conservative instinct in all of us is naturally pleased that there are so few changes recommended; yet, on second thought, can anyone deny a degree of danger in it too? Familiar names can sometimes lead to deeper pitfalls than novel ones. For instance, won't it be easy, too easy, for the synods of the future to be misled by the mere fact that they are called by the old-time name into overlooking or forgetting that their powers will be very different and more limited in the new order of things?

Fry's musing reluctance concerning the title of the chief executive did not carry over to his comments about the name "Executive Council": "We shall never again have to argue, either inside ourselves or among ourselves, in how far the Executive *Board* is a *board.* . . . Executive Council will be clearer as well as more distinctive." One argument, not mentioned by Fry, which carried weight with members of the delegations was that the executive officer was elected for a limited term of office and might possibly serve for a limited time only. For them the name "bishop" conveyed the idea of a lifetime title and function.

\* \* \*

The name of the new church itself stirred up considerable interest. Suggestions were legion and they gave expression to traditional preferences and predilections. Even the legal committee got into the act with a list of names that were out of bounds and a list of nominations that were acceptable. This great multitude of proposals today seem as irrelevant as the solid advice of grandparents for the naming of a new baby appears to be on the day after the baptism. One attribute did have a solid foundation in history and theology, however. For many of the immigrant churches the name "evangelical" or "evangelical-Lutheran" was highly treasured. Not only was it firmly rooted in history but it conveyed a testimony to the content of the church's message. "Evangelical" was gospel-centered and it excluded ideas and practices alien to the Lutheran tradition. So, even though "Evangelical-Lutheran" was a long middle name, it had fervent backing. It had one handicap, however; even twenty years ago it was becoming evident that the word "evangelical" was being appropriated by a type of revivalistic church effort with which the Lutheran church, at least that branch of it which formed the consensus of the JCLU, did not wish to be associated. The defense therefore lagged.

After two years of discussion the Commission arrived at a decision. On December 12, 1959, it adopted the name Lutheran Evangelical Church in America. The decision was short-lived, for the name immediately became unpopular. Its syllables twisted the tongue and its acronym was already causing cryptic remarks. When the Commission met in February 1960 the vote to reconsider was therefore readily adopted. A straw vote produced more evidence of uncertainty, with LECA and ELCA emerging in a tie with twelve votes each.  LCA, the dark horse, had nine, AELC had four (no great loyalty here), and seven others had one vote each.  What happened at that New York meeting is beyond documentation, but some sort of persuasion turned thirty of the forty-five votes in the next straw ballot to LCA, and a formal ballot soon made it official. The name was LUTHERAN CHURCH IN AMERICA.

*  *  *

From the early sessions of the Commission the location of the offices of the new church was a matter of contention.  The three smaller churches were inclined by geography to favor a location in the center of the country, Minneapolis being the headquarters city of Augustana.  The ULCA favored its traditional centers on the East Coast.  The confrontation was to some extent that of distance versus population density.  Chicago, Minneapolis, or even Detroit were more accessible from the far reaches of the church, but more than half the membership of the new church lived east of Pittsburgh. The tug-of-war was conducted in a polite and formal fashion, but the heaviest anchorman was on the eastern team.  To counteract any influence that Chicago might have through the familiarity bred by almost all the commission sessions, meetings were scheduled in Minneapolis and New York.  Expenses for the New York meeting were paid by the JCLU, in contrast to all other sessions where the individual churches covered the expenses of their delegates.  This generosity meant that the ULCA paid 80 percent of the expenses, and the gift was gratefully accepted by the other churches.  It had no influence on the vote, but the decision on headquarters was made at the New York meeting.  It had to be, for the time was February 1960 and the constitution had to be ready for the summer conventions.

A Committee on Headquarters reported for the first time in October 1959, distributing a study by James Mason entitled "On the Geographic Location of a Centralized Denominational Headquarters."  It met again in January 1960 and readied a massive report that was presented to the Commission meeting in New York in February.  The report starts out with four general criteria proposed by Mason:

1. natural kinship with the historical and geographic patternings of the denomination's supporting constituency and its affiliated agencies.

2. relationship to regional patterns of population and economic growth, social and economic function, and established lines of communication and transportation.

3. relationship through proximity and/or accessibility to Lutheran organizational centers as well as the wider Christian community.

4. social and cultural compatibility with the local environment.

In the analysis of these points the committee stressed, under point 1, the predominant population concentration in the eastern areas. The second point, the committee found, did "not clearly demonstrate an advantage for either city under consideration." Point 3, it was stated, carried two arguments, the one in favor of proximity to the centers of other Lutheran churches, although "there has been no demonstrated historical reason for believing that proximity of one headquarter to another has enhanced union conversations. . . . On the other hand to withdraw from the existing ecumenical relationships in the wider Christian community, which New York City provides, would tend to say that this church declares itself to be less concerned than it now is with these relationships." The last point stressed the advantage of New York in relation to the rest of the world, missionaries, visitors, students, mission and relief services, and so on.

An argument in favor of the New York location was the existence of a Church House, owned by the ULCA and, as a matter of course, visited by the Commission. In the end opposition to New York collapsed, in part because the influential Pension Board was located in the Augustana stronghold of Minneapolis. Chicago, which had no fervent backers, was given the headquarters of the Board of Home Mission in the acknowledgment that the heavy investment of effort would be made from this hub of transportation. Philadelphia, with its publication house, was a natural location for the Board of Publication and the church paper, so New York's eastern monopoly was somewhat modified. Parish Education was deemed to be a cousin of the publication activity and Youth Work was classified as a second cousin of both, so they were assigned to Philadelphia. Church Women also stayed in the City of Brotherly Love, but all other activities were centered in New York with, of course, the office of the president, the financial and the secretarial offices, and the convening site of the Executive Council being the core of central administration.

*  *  *

The seal of the church should be an eye-catching symbol and it must therefore be meaningful, appropriate, and pleasing to the eye. Symbols are representative of a reality and must not be misleading. A Committee on Seals therefore worked carefully, enlisting the skill of a professional artist. At the New York meeting in February 1960 two designs were presented, each with a central emphasis on the cross. The one was traditional, somewhat massive with Gothic lettering, with a decorative vine as background and with a cluster of grapes, symbolizing fruits, as the heart and center. The other was called contemporary, with a more open and airy design. Its symbols were simply a slender cross with the branches of a vine springing from the foot of the cross as from "the root of Jesse." The second, or contemporary, design won the favor and it is now well known to all members of the church.

*  *  *

Two considerations were obvious from the very beginning of the merger consultations as they related to the Canadian churches. The one was that the merger should be accomplished in such a way that decisions, especially in regard to nomenclature, were not discriminatory, discourteous, or restrictive to the Canadian Lutherans. The other was that the door should be left wide open for the Canadian churches to pursue the efforts already initiated toward the establishment of a Canadian Lutheran Church. A Committee on Canadian Matters was appointed, consisting of A. G. Jacobi (ULCA), Otto Olson (Augustana), and Alex Koski (Suomi). Johannes Knudsen was appointed to represent the JCLU on the committee in order to assure the Canadians of concern and full cooperation, and he convened the committee. Meetings were held in Winnipeg on September 11, 1958, and in Maywood on February 18, 1959. The work of fashioning recommendations was done entirely by the Canadians as they envisioned their task. Olson and Jacobi prepared the first report in a meeting at Winnipeg on October 28, 1958, and Olson presented it to the JCLU.

The report proceeded on the basis of two major assumptions: (1) that the work of the JCLU was not completed in regard to Canada, and (2) that the committee was speaking for a majority of Canadian Lutherans. The report expressed appreciation that the committee was established and it stated frankly at the outset that "the time is rapidly approaching when there should be established an autonomous, indigenous Lutheran Church in Canada." Merger negotiations were not regarded as a hindrance but as a "golden opportunity." The reasons for a Canadian church are: (1) Canada is an individual nation, related to but different from the United States; (2) "Without autonomy the Lutheran Church in Canada is a foreign church. . . . As long as we are not a Lutheran Church of Canada, we are by default an American Lutheran Church in Canada"; (3) Other Lutherans have seen the need for a United Canadian church with the possibility of representing both the Missouri Synod and the ALC; (4) "At least two of our churches have taken official action indicating a recognition that all Lutherans in Canada, at least someday, ought to be united in a national church." Furthermore, the report stated, both the ULCA and Augustana had formally encouraged the formation of a Canadian Lutheran Church, and "exploratory conversations looking forward to the possible establishment of 'one indigenous Lutheran Church in Canada' are in progress, and representatives of all major Lutheran bodies with congregations in Canada have been participating in these discussions for the past three years." Out of this may come a church consisting of either the churches now engaged in the JCLU merger plans or a combination of these with the ALC or with the ALC and Missouri.

The committee posited two alternatives for the current planning, one a single synod for the merged church in Canada, the other "a federation of the four synods currently being recommended by JCLU." The report discussed the practical functions of the alternate plans and concluded with a statement here quoted in part:

We trust that no one will feel that any portion of our report is motivated by unkindness or malice or dissatisfaction concerning the intention of JCLU or of our Churches for Canada. We are satisfied that the intention for Canada is always the best and that there is willingness to do more for Canada than we in Canada have any reason to expect by virtue of our size or importance in relation to the rest of the Church. At the same time we must confess that we believe that needs and problems have not always been rightly understood by those who have moved primarily in America.

We want it known that we fully realize that we will suffer loss by whatever extent ties with the "parent body" are severed. For many of us the ties with the American side have been very close and dear. At the same time we feel constrained to say that there will be compensating gains, as Lutheran Canadians become better acquainted with one another and as we undertake for ourselves the task given us by our Lord.

At the JCLU meeting in November 1958 it was decided to form a "Canada Section" with specified powers later spelled out in the new constitution. In response the Committee on Canadian Matters, meeting on February 18, 1959, stated that "a substantial portion . . . still favor one synod for Canada" but that "it would not request that consideration of this matter be reopened by JCLU." The committee made five suggestions, mostly in regard to nomenclature, but also suggesting two Home Mission regional secretaries for Canada and the constitutional authority for the Canadian Section to be incorporated under a Dominion Charter.

The final result was a Canada Section spelled out in Article XX of the constitution.

Section 1. The synods of this church located in Canada shall jointly constitute the Lutheran Church in America—Canada Section, through which they can speak with a united voice and act together in relationships and areas of church work in which there is a common Canadian concern.

Section 2. The Lutheran Church in America—Canada Section shall have full power, in the name and stead of this church:

a. To be incorporated under the laws of Canada.
b. To make approaches to, and have dealings with, the government of Canada and other Canadian authorities.
c. To form associations with Lutheran church bodies and other churches in Canada and to elect commissioners or representatives to such associations.

    d. To negotiate and consummate union with other Lutheran church
       bodies in Canada.
    e. To form at any time a separate and autonomous Lutheran Church
       in Canada.

Section 2 spelled out the functions and powers of the Canada Section in regard to conventions, officers, missions, publications, social programs, public relations activities, and other distinctive Canadian interests.

# 6. Congregations and Ministers

Two merger statements establish the basic role of congregations in the new church. One is Article IV in the LCA constitution, the article on membership. It reads in Section 1: "This church shall consist at its organization of the congregations and ministers of the [four churches of the merger]." The other statement was adopted by the JCLU at an early plenary session in March 1957. It reads: "A basic premise regarding congregations is that they shall be congregations of the general body and of a constituent unit."

In regard to the latter statement the early documents of the JCLU record an interesting variance. The Committee on Powers and Functions first formulated the statement at a meeting on February 15, 1957, prior to the above-mentioned plenary session, and in the form adopted by the committee the statement reads that congregations shall be congregations of the general body "through their relation to the constituent unit." The committee retained this version in its report of a meeting on June 24, 1957, even though the Commission had adopted something else in March.

There was no doubt in the minds of the Commission members, however, about the basic importance of the congregations. In March 1959 it adopted Article IV in the constitution and this article is unchanged to this day. It deals with "The Nature of the Church," and it reads in Section 2:

> The Church exists both as an inclusive fellowship and as local congregations gathered for worship and Christian service. Congregations find their fulfillment in the universal community of the Church, and the universal Church exists in and through congregations. This church, therefore, derives its character and powers both from the sanction and representation of its congregations and from its inherent nature as an expression of the broader fellowship of the faithful. In length, it acknowledges itself to be in the historic continuity of the communion of saints; in breadth, it expresses the fellowship of believers and congregations in this our day.

The strong emphasis upon the foundational importance of the congregation emerged even more strongly in the second draft of the constitution, the one that was not recorded in the appendixes to the minutes of the plenary sessions. Its proposed Article VI, on congregations, reads in Section 1:

As divinely instituted units of the Church of Christ, to which the Means of Grace have been committed, congregations of the *(name of church)* retain autonomy in all matters that they have not assigned to the *(name of church)* in this constitution or by other enactments.

This statement was toned down in the fourth draft of the constitution, the first one recorded with the minutes, but the emphasis on autonomy remains.

Congregations of this church retain authority in all matters that have not been committed to the *(name of church)* in this constitution or by other enactments.

This version remained intact with one significant addition, namely, the inclusion of synodical authority. The constitution as adopted in 1962 reads:

Congregations of this church retain authority in all matters that have not been committed to the Lutheran Church in America or its synods in this constitution or by subsequent enactments.

If the matter of autonomy and authority was not settled very specifically in the official documents, the function of the congregations was spelled out in great detail with an article in the constitution, a section in the by-laws of the LCA, an article in the approved constitution for synods, and a complete approved constitution of their own. It is not possible to discuss the details of their functions in this presentation, but one matter must be mentioned which caused considerable debate in the JCLU and which has caused even more debate since then. It has to do with membership.

In the Approved Constitution for Congregations there is mention of three types of membership: child members, adult or confirmed members, and communing members. A fourth category, contributing members, was proposed to the Commission, but it was not included. The problem has to do with the category of confirmed members which functions both in the spiritual realm of worship and in the quite secular realms of statistics and finance    Article IV, Section 4, in the Approved Constitution for Congregations read as it was adopted in 1962:

> Any confirmed member who, despite pastoral care and counseling, has failed for a period of three years to receive Holy Communion and to make any contribution of record to the congregation shall be classified by the church council as not in good standing (and shall be removed from the roll of confirmed members).    He shall be restored by the church council to the roll of confirmed members in good standing when he again receives the Lord's Supper and enters once more upon the other rights and obligations of a member of this congregation.

There was strong opposition among some of the Commission members, notably in the AELC, to the inclusion of any pressure or obligation for participation in Communion.    For them it was a matter of principle that participation in the sacrament was a concern of the individual in his relation to God and that it was not a matter of discipline by the church.    Particularly was there opposition to the removal of anyone from the roll of confirmed members, and this resulted in making that clause optional.    It was only when the emphasis on "pastoral care and counseling" was made introductory to the section that many delegates reluctantly concurred.    Had it not been for the repeated assurance that this was not a legalistic matter but a matter of pastoral concern, there might have been an insurmountable obstacle to union in this issue.    Other delegates, for whom the matter of required attendance and discipline had been a tradition, felt differently about this, of course.

The Achilles' heel of the matter and that which has caused repeated dissatisfaction lies not so much in varying opinions about discipline, however, as in another consequence.    The trouble comes from the confusion of the spiritual and the practical life of the congregation and its members.    According to the JCLU documents a confirmed member is not only a participant in the worship life of the congregation; he is also the basic unit for calculating financial obligations.    In the Approved Constitution for Synods, Article XII, Section 4, it is stated:

> The total sum of the budget . . . shall be apportioned by the Executive Board to the congregation on the basis of two factors: confirmed membership in good standing and congregational current expenses.

Besides the agony of those who suffer when they cannot discipline and even punish recalcitrant and noncommuning members of the congregation, it is the fiscal requirement that causes pain.  If an individual goes to Communion, he is considered to be a confirmed member of the congregation, even when he does not contribute to its budget.  The congregation must then include her or him in the number of units used for apportionment of the contribution to the synod.  Why, it is asked, should the faithful pay a greater share because a communing but fiscally unfaithful member is part of the statistics?

The malady arises from a far-reaching theological inadequacy in which the worshiping community and its human structure are confused.  The agony of this situation could have been avoided if another category of membership had been included, namely, a "contributing member," whose statistics had nothing to do with the spiritual life but was merely a matter of financial bookkeeping.  Then the matter of the relationship of members to the worship life of the congregation could have remained a matter of "pastoral care and counseling," especially if such care and counseling was not limited to the minister.  That the agony can be avoided even now by a modicum of human tolerance and compassion is another matter.

*    *    *

A basic premise of the proposed united church is that all ministers shall be, and shall be recognized as being, ministers of the church as a whole.  The general body shall define the standards of admission into and continuation in the ministry; these standards are to be applied and administered by the constituent units of the church.

On the recommendation of the Committee on Powers and Functions this resolution was adopted by the plenary session of the JCLU in March 1957 "as showing the present direction of thought of the Joint Commission on Lutheran Unity."  It gives expression first of all to a strong recognition of the significance of the ministry in the church, a significance that was further expressed in Article III of the constitution, which declares that the church consists of congregations and ministers.  Secondly it makes clear that the ministry of the coming church is not to be restricted by synodical jurisdiction.  If a person is accepted for ordination and service in one synod, he or she is thereby accepted in all.

The second paragraph in the March 1957 resolution of "present direction of thought" concerns the supervision of the ministry:

> The constituent units of the church shall be charged by its constitution with primary responsibility in the matters of
>
> a. recruiting, approval and supervision of candidates for the ministry, including any necessary beneficiary aid, and
>
> b. ordination, reception and discipline of ministers, and removal from the ministerial roll of men [sic!] who have left the office and functions of the ministry.
>
> Constituent units shall be recognized as acting for the general body in discharging these responsibilities.
>
> Men under discipline in one constituent unit must be restored by it to good standing before becoming eligible to acceptance in another constituent unit.

As is well known, the "present direction of thought" in March 1957 became the permanent and consistent directive for function in the new church.

All details of ministerial function cannot be discussed here, but certain important elements must be illuminated as they were given shape by the Commission. Before these are discussed, however, a major question must be asked: What is a minister? To this question the official documents prepared by the JCLU give no answer. The ministry is nowhere defined. Even when the question is expanded to include the confessional documents of the church there is no specific answer. There are many statements about the function of the ministry but no delineation of what it is. This is not necessarily a weakness or a handicap. The ministry is established and accepted through early and long tradition and through the worship life of the contemporary church. It involves human relations and human functions but it is also, and primarily, a mediation of the worship life with God. To define it sharply in documentary, and thereby human, terms can infringe upon the mystery of its essential nature. That subsequent bureaucracy has dared to step into this situation to define the ministry in terms of its secular function underscores the wisdom of the JCLU in its refusal to attempt such a definition.

It might thus be recognition of the fact that we speak God's wisdom in mystery (1 Cor. 2:7) that lies behind the sparseness with which the LCA constitution introduces the article on ministry.

Without elaboration the statements are simple and functional assertions of qualification and performance, and they were so formulated from the very first draft. Article VII, Sections 1–3, with only the first sentence of Section 2 quoted, reads:

> This church shall define the standards of acceptance into and continuance in its ministry. These standards shall be applied and administered by the synods.
>
> Ordination and reception of ministers shall be a function of the synods, acting in behalf of this church.
>
> Each minister shall conform his preaching and teaching to the Confession of Faith of this church and shall lead a life befitting his holy office.

It has already been shown how the constitution delegates the supervision, or shepherding, of ministers to the synods. The by-laws add a lengthy series of functional regulations, five and a half pages in fact, to the canon about ministers. The bulk of these regulations is found in the by-laws, Section II, Item 13, which states: "To assure full equity and protection of the rights both of the individual concerned and of his church, the procedure in cases of discipline of ministers shall be as follows." The procedures are too lengthy to be included here, but they can be read as evidence of the personal and sensitive nature of the ministry, perhaps also as an awareness of the evidence for historical abuses.

Section 4 of Article VII demands attention, both for the discussion it precipitated in the JCLU and for the current reaction to it.

> After the organization of the Lutheran Church in America no person, who belongs to any organization which claims to possess in its teachings and ceremonies that which the Lord has given solely to His Church, shall be ordained or otherwise received into the ministry of this church, nor shall any person so ordained or received by this church be retained in its ministry if he subsequently joins such an organization. Violation of this rule shall make such minister subject to discipline.

Behind this statement lies a history and a debate.

The question of membership in "secret organizations or lodges" arose early in the plenary sessions and its was referred to the Committee on Doctrine and Living Tradition. This committee received the problem with reluctance, inasmuch as it did not regard it as a doctrinal matter, but it came up with position papers from each of the four churches. Writing for the AELC, Axel Kildegaard states

that his church had an antilodge tradition, particularly at the turn
of the century, but that the question is now dormant.  It was his
opinion "that our pastors are almost unanimously opposed to such
orders and would be agreeable to a requirement that no pastor be
allowed to hold any such membership.  Such a requirement, however, should not be based upon doctrinal grounds."  Walter Kukkonen, writing for Suomi, explains the problems and ambiguities of
his church's relation to a Finnish lodge where it has never been
determined whether the lodge "does in fact incorporate religion in
its teachings and ceremonies."  He states, however, that Suomi cannot but ask for provisions in the constitution which will make it
impossible for ministers to compromise their faith.  Augustana, as
reported by Karl Mattson, had a constitutional ban against ministerial membership in "any organization whose teachings or practices
conflict with those of the Church," and it requests that similar
qualifications be adopted by the new church.  He agonizes about
the problem of double standards for clergy and laity and begs that
the question not be approached legalistically, claiming that it is a
problem of church order and not of doctrine.  T. A. Kantonen, writing for the ULCA, quotes that church's constitutional claim "to
advise and admonish concerning association and affiliation with non-
ecclesiastical and other organizations whose principles and practices
appear to be inconsistent with full loyalty to the Christian Church,
but the Synods alone shall have the power of discipline."  He raises
the question of the rejection of an organization through strict interpretation of formal statements in contrast to "actual experience,"
"when a man's fraternal affiliation represents only social and philan-
thropic interests."  He also raises the question of discrimination
between ministry and the laity.  Asking about the proper method to
deal with all this, he states that "the method generally used in the
ULCA is to admonish and advise rather than to coerce."

The discussion in the Commission on December 13, 1957, was
warm.  It was soon clarified that consensus opinion rejected the
Donatist position that this was an ethical concern.  Consequently
there was also consensus that this was a functional matter, a matter
of order or a problem of divided loyalty for the person who was to
serve the whole congregation in its worship relation to God.  The

concern that divided the Commission had to do with the alternatives of admonition or ban, and this became the one instance in which the count of votes had decisive significance.  Let the minutes of the plenary session tell the story.  After parliamentary sparring and lengthy debate, which lasted into the evening hour, the minutes read:

> Motion was then adopted, by a vote of 23 for and 10 against, referring to the Committee on Powers and Functions, for inclusion in substance, the original statement as amended:
>
> "If the church shall be free to advise and admonish concerning association and affiliation with organizations which claim to possess in their teachings and ceremonies that which the Lord has given solely to His church, its ministry must not be compromised by pastors who belong to such organizations.  Provision shall be made in the constitution of the church whereby ministers ordained by the new church shall agree to refrain from membership in such organizations or be subject to discipline."
>
> Following this action Dr. Fry requested a recess of ten minutes for a caucus of the ULCA Commission.  Following the recess Dr. Fry presented the following statement: "As a concession in love to the living tradition of our sister churches, the Commission of the ULCA acquiesces unanimously in the vote just taken."  It was agreed that this statement be entered in the minutes of this meeting.

\* \* \*

A final word concerning congregations and ministers should be said in regard to Article III of the LCA constitution, the article on membership.  Section 1 reads:

> This church shall consist at its organization of the congregations and ministers of the American Evangelical Lutheran Church, of the Augustana Evangelical Lutheran Church, of The Finnish Evangelical Lutheran Church of America, and of the constituent synods of The United Lutheran Church in America.

This statement combines congregation and ministers as basic entities or constituent units of the church.  This was not an innovation, for a similar statement was found in the constitutions of the AELC, Augustana, and Suomi.  It was not found in the constitution of the ULCA, although it was in the historic background of this church that the idea and practice had first arisen.

The combination of congregations and ministers is a creation of pioneer times and it is in that situation that it has its justification. It appeared first when German Lutherans in Pennsylvania were finding their way together in the 1740s, and their ways set a pattern for others, a precedent that was repeated time and again. As representatives of their homeland churches in Europe, pastors followed the people into a new land. They preached for the settlers and helped them form congregations. When these newly constituted fellowships sought contact and fellowships with each other, the ministers took the initiative and usually constituted the first joint efforts. Eventually congregations sent delegates to the "ministerium," but these delegates did not replace the ministers; they joined them. As a result the organizations became associations of ministers and congregations and they were called synods. Not only was the "synodical" organization practical and justified but it was probably the only manner in which a common effort could be maintained in pioneer times. The precedent having been set, however, it became an indigenous institution. Churches founded as late as the second half of the nineteenth century adopted the traditional American example, and the commonly used name for a church was "synod." This is a curious concept of the church, however, which is hard to defend except on historical grounds, and it has no parallel outside North America. There are important reasons for saying that people constitute the church or that congregations do. For Roman Catholics and Episcopalians it makes sense to say that office (or order) constitutes the church. But where can one find theological justification or non-American precedent for the combination of ministers and congregations? Scripture offers no help, nor does early church history. Logically there is no way in which congregations and ministers can be juxtaposed or made parallel. Practically speaking, this combination gives the ministry a weight and voice in the decisions of the church which for some seem out of proportion to its significance and not in harmony with the basic nature of its office.

# 7. Seminaries and Colleges

The problem of ownership and control of the theological seminaries of the proposed church proved to be a knotty and even divisive one. It was a matter of overabundance and a possible reduction of numbers. The ULCA had ten seminaries, including two in Canada, and they were owned and administered by the synods. There was a great deal of tradition and loyalty related to these institutions, particularly the older ones, and they were a matter of sectional pride. It would be a difficult matter to move them or to reduce their number. The other churches had one seminary each, and these institutions were also regarded with loyalty and pride as expressions of traditional values. Concurrently with the merger of churches, however, these churches had taken the initiative to merge their seminaries. Grand View Seminary of the AELC and Suomi Seminary moved to Maywood, Illinois, and joined Chicago Lutheran Theological Seminary (ULCA). At the same time as the merger meetings in the JCLU, these three seminaries entered negotiations with Augustana Seminary, Rock Island, Illinois, and the merger of the four seminaries into one, for the time being on two campuses, was consummated at the same time as the merger of the churches. A strong sentiment was thereby engendered that inasmuch as the three churches had taken such sacrificial steps toward the solution of the overabundance and duplication of seminaries, a similar move of cooperation and goodwill should be forthcoming from the ULCA. The practical aspect of this was the matter of ownership and control. Should the seminaries be owned and controlled by the synods, as had been the practice in the ULCA, or should they be owned and controlled by the national church, as had been the practice in the three other churches?

The Joint Commission took the first step toward the confrontation and solution of the issue at its initial session in December 1956,

when it appointed the Committee on Powers and Functions to prepare studies as guidance for further planning. This committee met
on January 10 and February 15, 1957, but it barely dented the matter
of seminaries by saying: "In this area there are two views: general
body ownership and constituent body ownership for which further
study is needed." At its meeting on March 9, 1957, the JCLU pursued the matter further and moved a step toward solution by
expressing as "the present direction of thought" on the matter that
"ownership and primary responsibility for administration and control of theological seminaries shall be vested in the constituent units
of the united church" and "that the general body shall have a major
board, or division of a board, with the following powers: a. Construct a master plan of location of seminaries, b. Approve the establishment and relocation of seminaries within the united church," and
offering suggestions about curriculum, finances, scholarships, faculty,
board members, and so on. The stage was hereby already set for
the eventual compromise, namely, that the synods should own and
administer the seminaries but that the general church body should
determine their location.

That "the present direction of thought" had not gained Augustana's approval became evident when the Committee on Powers and
Functions met on November 2, 1957, with the AELC member
absent. On behalf of the Executive Council of Augustana Church,
Oscar Benson, the president of the church, offered a substitute for
the statement adopted in March. In this motion to substitute, the
secondary and trailing items were much like the JCLU's statement,
but the first points read thus:

1. Ownership and primary responsibility for administration and control of theological seminaries shall be vested in the church.

2. The church shall have a major board, whose authority shall be to
   establish and maintain standards for and a program of theological
   education in the church as stipulated below. There shall also be
   regional boards . . . which shall have the responsibility for institutional administration of the respective seminaries subject to the
   authority and direction of the general board of theological education.

The terse record of the minutes spells out the drama. "Motion to substitute was defeated by vote of four to three, the chairman breaking the tie." The minutes continue:

Dr. Benson gave notice that the substitute would be reported to the JCLU in December 19, 1957 as a minority report.

Dr. Fry then moved

that if the action of this committee is supported by JCLU, the committee records its readiness to continue restudy of the former plan for theological education with the intention of strengthening it in the direction of increased influence and control of theological education on the part of the general body.

The motion was unanimously adopted.

The confrontation of views was continued at the JCLU meeting on December 12, 1957. Again the bare language of the minutes spells out the story of what happened.

*Motion* presented and seconded that the Commission approve the action of the majority of the Sub-committee in defeating a substitute offered by the Augustana Church's members on the Sub-committee to take the place of earlier action of the Joint Committee on Lutheran Unity concerning theological education.

A *substitute* for this motion was adopted: "that we ask the Sub-committee to restudy the former plan for theological education with the intention of strengthening it in the direction of increased influence and control on the part of the general body.

A forty-five minute discussion of principle followed the vote.

The first confrontation, on the direct question of ownership and control of the seminaries, was now over, and the decision had quickly gone to those who favored synodical control. But the battle of reduction was not yet over. A new front was formed and the issue became the matter of deciding the location of individual seminaries in the merger commission *before the merger.* The majority had agreed to a so-called master plan of location, but the question was now whether those who favored a decision by the JCLU could use the leverage of the situation to determine locations *before the final merger action* or whether the matter would be passed on in an unresolved state to the new church. The first step toward this end came in March 1958 when the JCLU adopted a recommendation from the Committee on Powers and Function., with certain amendments. The main items of the resolution read as follows:

I. Responsibility for ownership and administration of theological seminaries shall reside in the synods, which shall elect the governing boards of seminaries.

II. A table showing which seminaries shall be related to which synods shall be submitted by the Joint Commission on Lutheran Unity to the first convention of the ——— Church for its action, said table to have received previous approval by the merging churches.

III. The ——— Church shall have a board (or division) of theological education with powers defined as follows:

A. To recommend to the convention of the Church for its action:

1. A master plan of location and of possible areas of specialization of the theological seminaries;

2. Proposals for establishment and relocation of theological seminaries;

3. Revisions of the table showing which seminaries shall be related to which synods.

In November 1958 the JCLU appointed a new committee, hereafter known as the Committee on Seminaries. This committee was given the matter of alignment of seminaries to synods and the task of designing a master plan. It took steps to involve all the existing seminaries in the matter of alignment, but on June 8–9, 1959, it met with the seminaries participating in the Chicago merger to study the matter of a new location and by midsummer it had yet no plans for alignment. At the July 1959 meeting of the JCLU, Oscar Benson made an attempt to force the issue on the number of seminaries. He introduced a motion as the expression of the Ecumenical Committee of the Augustana Church that "JCLU enunciate the principle that the new Church operate and support a maximum of five or six seminaries." The motion was deferred to the December 1959 meeting of the JCLU, but at that meeting the minutes record that "by common consent the Augustana motion was now withdrawn."

At this December 1959 meeting P. O. Bersell presented the report from the Committee on Seminaries and the JCLU adopted the following motion:

That the Committee on Seminaries be instructed to prepare and present to the February, 1960 meeting of JCLU:

1. A provisional table of alignment of synods and theological seminaries to be in effect during the first biennium of the new church, and

2. A projection for the future of the number and location of the theological seminaries of the new church to be presented to its constituting convention for commendation to the Board of Theological Education as it constructs the master plan which it be the duty of that board to present to the second convention of the church.

Already there was talk of implementation, not at the merger convention but at "the second convention of the church."

On January 19–20, 1960, the Committee on Seminaries made a major effort to gather data and opinions on the questions of seminary locations and alignment. It invited representatives of all the seminaries plus representatives of synods and conferences to a meeting in Chicago. On the first day it organized itself with P. O. Bersell as chairman and Franklin Clark Fry as secretary. The other members were Ralph Jalkanen and Ronald Jespersen. A paper was read by Bersell and one by Robert Mortvedt, who at that time served as executive secretary for the theological boards of Augustana as well as the ULCA. The committee adopted a statement of guidelines for the conference on the following day.

It is the intention of the Seminary Committee to include in its report to JCLU on the fulfillment of its mandate a mention of the specific situations possibly involving seminary relocations or combinations to which the Board of Theological Education of the Lutheran Evangelical [sic] Church in America should give special consideration in connection with the construction of the master plan of theological education for the new church.

A considerable amount of data and opinion came out of the meeting on January 20, much too much even to summarize here, and it is available in the report to the JCLU appended to plenary sessions.

After the day-long seminar the Committee on Seminaries wrote a report for the JCLU which ended with the following paragraph:

The committee lists here the following questions and situations that in its judgment ought to be examined by the Board of Theological Education:

1. Merger of Augustana Seminary, Chicago Seminary (Maywood), Suomi Seminary and Grand View Seminary into a single institution located in Chicago or environs.

2. Possible combination of Gettysburg and Philadelphia seminaries.

3. Possible combination of Northwestern Seminary with the new seminary in or near Chicago.

4. Possible combination of Hamma Divinity School (Springfield, Ohio) with the new seminary in or near Chicago.

5. Possible relocation of Central Seminary (Fremont, Nebraska) or combination with the new seminary in or near Chicago.

6. The optimum and maximum desirable size of a theological seminary.

In addition the committee issued a statement entitled "Principles Governing the Number, Location and Alignment of Theological Seminaries in the Lutheran Evangelical Church in America." The bulk of the document had to do with academic requirements and with faculty, location and property, library, tuition, constituency, and cooperation with other Lutherans. But the first three items read:

1. It is agreed that, at the organization of the LECA, all the theological seminaries of the merging church bodies and their constituent synods shall be recognized by the LECA as institutions of the church. During the first biennium of the church and thereafter, they shall be under the oversight of the Board of Theological Education in accordance with the constitution and by-laws of the church and its synods.

2. Each seminary shall, during the first biennium, receive direct financial support from the synods to which it is aligned, in accordance with the attached table of synodical alignments. Financial provision will be made in the first budget of the church to assure each seminary of as much income from church sources during each year of the first biennium of the LECA as that seminary received from its supporting constituency in the last year preceding the merger.

3. During the first biennium, no major investment in land or buildings should be made by any seminary except by approval of the supporting synods and the Board of Theological Education.

The committee also issued a table of provisional alignment of seminaries and synods.

This report was submitted to the JCLU session in February 1960, and the Commission approved the Statement of Principles with the exception of a paragraph about reporting, for which it substituted a motion "that JCLU recommend to the constituting convention of the church that the Board of Theological Education be instructed to report to the second convention of the church on the master plan for theological seminaries." The Commission also approved of the "Table of Provisional Alignment of Synods and Seminaries for the First Biennium," but T. A. Kantonen and Carl C. Rasmussen recorded their votes in opposition to this. The Commission then agreed that the table of suggested alignment be submitted to the cooperating churches at their conventions to be held during the summer.

The summer following the above-mentioned meeting of the JCLU was the summer of the church conventions at which the first ratification of the constitution took place. When the Commission met in March 1961, however, the Committee on Seminaries reported only on its involvement in the fiscal problems of the merged seminary in Chicago, whether the new church should cover the income which Augustana had previously received from its church. The committee recommended support for the transition period. There was nothing in the report about the master plan, and the committee took no further steps to resolve the issue, which seemed to be settled by default. The result of all the debate was that the JCLU did not come up with a master plan for location of seminaries. It passed the problem on to the new church. In the Bulletin of Reports to the Constituting Convention, Recommendation 29, the outcome is reflected in the abandonment of any attempt to settle the matter before the merger convention. The recommendation reads:

That the Board of Theological Education be instructed to report to the convention of the church in 1964 on the master plan for theological seminaries which is called for in Section X, G, 3 of the by-laws, which reads:

The board shall bring recommendation to the conventions, at its discretion, on:

a. A master plan of location and of possible areas of specialization of theological seminaries.

Recommendation 28 spelled out a provisional alignment of synods and seminaries, an alignment that became permanent.

* * *

Among the committees appointed by the JCLU, the Committee on College Education and Church Vocations stands out as a model of competent and comprehensive coverage. The trail of its effort and the conclusions of its research are easy to follow, for the committee issued a comprehensive final report on January 19, 1962, covering all the bases and the phases of its work, including a complete account of its meetings. The report is too comprehensive even to summarize here, and much of its information is highly factual. For historians of education in the Lutheran church the document is invaluable, and it is available in the LCA archives. Its highlights shall be given here.

The committee changed some of its members along the way, and the list of these will be found in the Appendix, but the original committee was appointed on March 7, 1959, and it was given the assignment "eventually to recommend to JCLU the alignment of colleges and synods on the basis of the colleges as they exist at the time of merger and not to concern itself with the possible merger and relocation of colleges except as the committee is specifically requested to do so. . . ." In one sense the committee task was uncomplicated. It was practical and rather sharply delineated, without theological complications. On the other hand it was vast and highly detailed. The four churches brought with them to the merger eighteen four-year colleges and four two-year colleges, and the synods to which these were to be related in the new church numbered thirty-two. In themselves these facts involve a great amount of data about tradition, geography, and finance. Relating them in a practical and harmonious way and capping the conglomerate with a unified central supervision was no small task. Under the direction of its chairman, Erling Jensen, and with the able consultation of Robert Mortvedt, who at that time served as executive secretary for higher education in both Augustana and the ULCA, the committee performed in exemplary manner.

Three purposes stand out in the proceedings:

1. To assure the church that its educational institutions functioned in conformity with the ideals and principles of the church.
2. To assure the institutions of a fair and adequate supportive base within the church.
3. To insure the sound financial existence of each institution.

The committee met nine times over a period of two-and-a-half years and some of its meetings were mass gatherings of a consultative nature, where all the institutions involved had an opportunity to report and be heard. It employed the know-how and skill of the boards and agencies of the four churches with their competent personnel, and it reached into other pan-Lutheran and national educational agencies for information and advice. The data it gathered and made available is a valuable resource for the historian, but it is not relevant for publication two decades later. Things have changed surprisingly in the meantime and the institutions have grown.

As a whole the committee, as well as the Commission, were concerned that the problems of transition were taken care of and that no college should suffer financially in the interim period. It was also concerned that the alignment of colleges to synods be fair over the long run. The details of this and their consequences can be read in the subsequent history of each college. A merger (Luther and Midland in Nebraska), a relocation (Carthage from Illinois to Wisconsin), and a move to independence (Hartwick), have taken place since the merger, but on the whole the structure has been continued as it was planned by the JCLU. A report on the interim and long-range arrangement for fiscal support of 1962 is unrealistic today and can only be read as another documentation of inflation.

Of lasting interest is a statement of principles from the committee:

### PRINCIPLES GOVERNING THE ALIGNMENT OF SYNODS AND COLLEGES

1. The ideal is that in the new Church all of the colleges will be *church-colleges* in the best sense of the word—colleges whose faculties, administrations, and boards seek to provide a quality education within the framework of the Gospel of Jesus Christ. Such institution are avowed champions of the Christian point of view.

2. All synods are urged to recognize and acknowledge the fact that the strength and vitality of the Church is intimately related to the strength and vitality of its program of higher education, including both colleges and seminaries.

3. The genius and history of an institution will be respected. In general, however, it will be assumed that an institution merits the support of the Church because it renders a recognized service commensurate with the investment that is being made in it. Institutions do not exist for themselves.

4. All synods are urged to think in terms of fully-accredited, respected,

and adequately-supported colleges in their respective categories. No attempts will be made to establish uniformity among the colleges of the Church. Institutions will be encouraged to become as strong as possible; and all reasonable efforts will be exerted to prevent colleges from becoming weak and ineffective.

5. All synods will stand in a supporting relationship to at least one college, even though a college of the Church may not be within their borders.

6. Every defensible step will be taken to provide each college with an adequate base of constituent and financial support, since it can clearly be demonstrated that constituent support and strength of institutions usually go hand in hand. The synod(s) aligned with a particular college shall include the synod in whose territory the college is located and the synod that supplies the largest percentage of the student enrollment to that particular college.

7. The Board of College Education and Church Vocations shall have a budget commensurate with its responsibility for a sound program of higher education, and it will be expected to give such guidance as it can in seeing that synodical support of colleges is shared in a manner beneficial to the entire educational program of the Church.

8. No college should suffer financially in consequence of the merger of the churches. In general, the minimum total of direct financial support, including grants from synods plus grants made through the Board of College Education and Church Vocations, should equal the financial support received by the college through synods, conferences, and Church at the time of merger. All cases, of course, must receive individual consideration.

The committee findings were expressed in Recommendation 30 to the Constituting Convention, regarding the alignment of colleges and synods, and in Recommendation 31, regarding counsel to the new synods on college support. Its input is otherwise absorbed in the provisions of the by-laws of the LCA, Section X, B. Item 2 reads:

The relations of this church to colleges shall be sustained entirely through the synods, except as specified hereinafter and in other ways proposed by the convention or by the Board of College Education and Church Vocations to which the synods concerned have in each case agreed.

Item 3. The Board of College Education and Church Vocations shall have the responsibility to:

a. Make recommendations to the convention, for its action, on the establishment and location of colleges.

b. Set standards, both of academic excellence and of church participation in their government and life, for recognition or continued recognition of colleges as related to the Lutheran Church in America or any of its synods.

c. Conduct studies, and give advice to colleges, on curricular offerings and standards.

d. Counsel related colleges on administrative and other matters as mutually agreed.

e. Grant supplementary financial aid to colleges at the discretion of the board and within the resources made available for that purpose by the Lutheran Church in America.

f. Act on detailed arrangements proposed by synods for their cooperation in colleges owned or conducted by other Lutheran church bodies.

# 8. Boards and Commissions

Twenty years later it is not difficult to visualize what the Commission on Lutheran Unity was trying to do in the manner of administration in the new church and why it was doing it; it is also very easy to be critical. If we are critical of its accomplishments, and we must have been critical inasmuch as the whole pattern was discarded after a decade of operation and replaced by a new structure, we must be generous enough to concede that our superior hindsight was not available in the 1950s. The JCLU administrative pattern was a drawing-board product which did not adequately foresee the overlappings and jurisdictional knots that soon developed. Whether the new design from the drawing boards of the late sixties and early seventies will prove to be more efficacious time will tell, and there is a great deal of difference between being "efficient" and being "efficacious." But hindsight should not tarnish too readily the dreams of the fifties. Those dreams envisioned a bright new city with paved streets, modern mansions, and functional lines of communications.

The postwar spirit of the fifties was featured by the joy of peace, the glow of new-found relations, the budding hopes of universal cooperation, and the trust in institutions of common effort and harmony, to wit, the United Nations, the World Council of Churches, and the Lutheran World Federation. For those who experienced the exuberance of Lund and Hannover and the new visions of church work, epitomized by the magic words "stewardship" and "evangelism," which America was bringing to the world, there is a balm of forgiveness for the sins of overexpectation and overcommitment. The spirit of the fifties was not the naive optimism of the nineteenth century, which would Christianize the world in a generation, but it was the flush of hope and trust in a new day. That day is now shrouded by Vietnam and Watergate; it is clouded by the growing and legitimate claims of an expanded world; and it is

78

dimmed by the fumes of the energy crisis.   Our age is more sophisticated, perhaps, and it is more realistic in its disillusionment, but is it yet wiser or less selfish?

Recent experience has taught Christians to probe more deeply into the nature of the church and its gospel and into the nature of created human living.   "Mission" has become a term difficult to use with the triumphant echoes of past claims ringing in our ears.   Yet mission has become a more profound and central concept, and even more than a concept and a practice.   Mission has become a challenge to the very life of the organized church.   It is a challenge to planned institutionalism, to bureaucratic dominance, to statistical criteria.   The Christian community must move beyond what was said and done in the exuberant fifties, yet it must also move beyond what was said and done in the skeptical years immediately behind us.   It must live with the gospel in its community of worship and try better to understand what this means in terms of human living.

There was no question in the fifties that a church institution had to have agencies in abundance in order to implement its objectives and programs.   The Joint Commission put this into constitutional words in Article XIII of the proposed, and adopted, constitution by talking about "major administrative units of this church which are charged with substantial segments of functional activity."   These units were to be called "boards" and they were to be incorporated separately.   The boards were not there to conduct completely independent policies.   They were to be "amenable in all things to the church" (Article XIII, Section 4); they were to be accountable to the conventions; they were subject to review by the Executive Council, which was to coordinate their efforts (Article XII, Section 3, h). But they were imposingly there.   Their number was large, eight in all, namely: American Missions, College Education and Church Vocations, Parish Education, Pensions, Publication, Social Ministry, Theological Education, and World Missions—in alphabetical order and not in order of importance—but the eight in the ark could not be saved through the deluge of structural reform.

There were also commissions, seven in number: Architecture; Church Papers; Evangelism; Press, Radio, and Television; Stewardship; Worship; Youth Activities.   Their number would have exceeded that of the boards if the "men" and "women" had not sought separate facilities. Commissions were "primarily of a study or service character" (Article XIV, Section 1) and they were to be under the supervision of the Executive Council (Article XII, Section 3, i). And then there were "common agencies," but these were not given constitutional status. The functions of the boards and commissions were spelled out in detail in the by-laws.

"Mission," in the profound sense of its significance as the heart of the gospel, was therefore not a new and different agenda item for the Commission. Undoubtedly it lived thus in the minds of many delegates, and there were disturbing signs on the horizon at home and abroad, challenging traditional institutionalism. The doubts about objectives and procedures had not emerged into specifics as yet, however, and the agenda of the tradition remained. American Missions was still an effort at multiplying and undergirding congregations; World Missions was still "the proclamation of the Gospel in word and deed and the administration of the Sacraments in behalf of this church" (By-laws, Section X, Item 1, a). An existential question facing the church in the seventies was thus delayed, and the green light was on for institutional proliferation. Lest this way of stating it be taken as criticism, let it be said that it is not thus intended. The motivations of the JCLU were genuine and the spirit was thoughtful; the world just had not moved beyond the corner of its next crisis.

A Committee on American Missions was appointed at the March 1957 meeting of the JCLU. Even before its appointment it had been given direction by a statement of the Committee on Powers and Functions dated January 1957: "We agree a plan should be evolved for the giving of considerable amount of initiative to the constituent units, but the strategy and direction is with the general body." The committee consisted of Richard H. Sorensen (chairman), E. H. List (secretary), Thorsten A. Gustafson, and Henry Kangas. Consultants were Donald L. Houser, R. A. Gerberding, and Theodore E. Mattson. The committee met on July 11, 1957, and August 19, 1957, reporting for the first time to the JCLU on September 19, 1957.

It was obvious from the start that the driving concern was the matter of organization. The first report proposed that there be a Board of American Missions (BAM) of the merged church with members elected by the church, and that the BAM should elect a staff of directors, secretaries, and regional directors (RD). It also proposed that each constituent unit (CU), as synods were yet called, should have an American Missions Committee (AMC). The report lapsed into almost esoteric acronymic lingo: "The AMC of each CU shall be responsible . . . to the BAM through the RD." The line of authority was clear, with the main responsibility lying in a national organization, carried out through regional directors in close cooperation with a corresponding synodical authority. That there was potential for friction through overlapping jurisdiction between regional directors and synodical officials, particularly in the calling of pastors, was clear, but apparently it was expected that mutual loyalty to a common cause and understanding attitudes on the part of personnel could avoid trouble. The financing was a centralized concern, however.

The emphasis on organization was strong; the objectives and purposes of the entire activity were apparently taken for granted. They appear almost casually in the organizational directives. "The development of missions shall be carried on by the BAM through Regional Directors (RD) in cooperation with the respective American Missions Committees (AMC) of the constituent units." So, missions were to be developed! "The AMC of each CU shall be responsible for finding fields. . . ." So, there was to be a search for fields! "The president of the CU shall recommend to the BAM through the RD an approved candidate for call as pastor of the mission congregation." So mission pastors were to be called!

The committee met again on November 20, 1957, and wrote a constitution for the proposed Board of American Missions, a constitution which was generally approved, although amended in a number of details, by the Commission in December. This document was also terse in regard to purposes, stating that the object of the board shall be "to establish, administer and support the work of Home Missions of the ——— Church," but the Commission dropped the word "establish." It was apparently taken for granted that "home missions" was a known and indisputable concept. The "duties, powers and functions" of the board were described as supervision and administration of home missions and as the power to call pastors and engage other workers. It was given authority to handle finances and departmentalize its work, being required to report to the executive "Board." In addition, the constitution and a set of by-laws specified in detail the organization of the board and its activities.

The early stages of planning having been completed, further action had to await the first adoption of the new constitution in the summer of 1960. An enlarged board then met in the fall of 1961 with N. Everett Hedeen as chairman and Richard H. Sorensen as secretary. In addition to the committee members and their consultants, eighteen "board nominees" were present. They were briefed by JCLU chairman Malvin H. Lundeen and by Martin E. Carlson about the duties of the board of the new church. Lundeen stated that the purpose of the meeting was to provide occasion for board members to get to know each other and to be informed about the program of the first biennium, but the board was not to make decisions of operation as yet. In a lengthy session much ground was covered. Donald L. Houser and Theodore E. Mattson described the work of the ULCA and Augustana, respectively, while Raymond W. Wargelin and Holger O. Nielsen presented that of Suomi and the AELC. Finances were discussed and many practical questions were aired. The committee now had a specific function, according to the new constitution, namely, "responsibility for leadership in and general supervision of the total program of American Missions in the Lutheran Church in America."

From this time on the activity of the committee consisted in practical arrangements for an immediate start of operations in the new church, including finances and the organization and lease of a new headquarters. At one point expectations for the new work were expressed in the agreement "that in the first year of operation 125 new congregations in normal situations should be developed, that work should be done in 125 urban or inner-city congregations, that 80 congregations would be involved in town and country work, that church extension work would be big business and require big business methods of operation, that work should be done amongst the

American Indians, that work should be done with migrants, that work should be done in college and university centers, that work should be done in military centers, that work should be done amongst immigrant groups, that work should be done in linguistic congregations, that much work needs to be done among Spanish speaking people, that work should be done in tourist and resort areas, that work should be done in senior citizen areas, that pioneer work should be done in pioneer areas, that work should be continued in the mountain missions." A heady and ambitious start!

The by-laws of the LCA state the objectives of American Missions as follows:

Section X.  A.  Board of American Missions

Item 2.  The Board of American Missions shall make effective provision in its structure and patterns of work to discharge its resp n i- bilities for

a. planning for, planting and servicing home mission congregations,

b. giving extension aid by means of expert counsel and through the operation of loan funds, and

c. conserving and strengthening urban and rural congregations confronting special problems.

The functions are named in item 6 as: finding fields, surveying fields, approving fields for occupancy, developing fields, providing parsonages, selecting church sites, selecting temporary places of worship, supplying initial equipment, organizing congregations, calling pastors, supporting pastors, and assisting established congregations confronting special problems.

*  *  *

As with American Missions the main concern about World Missions was organization and funding.  The name became "World Missions," as used by Augustana, in contrast to "Foreign Missions," as used by the ULCA.  "World Missions" had a more ecumenical ring, but the definition still concerned the area "outside the Dominion of Canada and the United States of America" (By-laws, Section X, Item I, a).  There was enough to take care of.  World War II had ravaged the mission work, and the planning spirit was naturally that of restoration.  It is indicative of the times that the JCLU documents speak yet of Tanganyika and not of Tanzania. All of the four churches had mission programs. Suomi had missions in Japan and Tanganyika, both of them cooperative efforts with other churches. The AELC had traditionally and strongly supported the Santal Mission in India in cooperation with the UELC and the churches of Norway and Denmark.

The most extensive work was that of Augustana and the ULCA. Augustana had missions in Tanganyika, independently and in cooperation with the National Lutheran Council. They had rescued the German mission work in what was formerly German East Africa. It also had cooperative work in Uruguay, Hong Kong, Taiwan, Japan, India, and North Borneo. The ULCA had missions, cooperatively and independently, in Argentina, Uruguay, British Guiana, Hong Kong, India, Japan, Liberia, Malaya, and Tanganyika. The efforts of the four churches joined together made an impressive and demanding list, and much work needed to be done to coordinate and continue the task.

The Committee on World Missions was appointed in March 1957, and it had also been given direction by the Committee on Powers and Functions in a January 10, 1957, statement: "We agree the functions and powers for mission shall be the prerogative of the general body." The committee met on July 10 in Minneapolis. It consisted of Earl Erb, Melvin Hammarborg, Mrs. Ernest D. Nielsen, Ralph Lundquist, J. E. Kunos, and Ralph Loew (chairman). "The purpose of the meeting was to explore the program of the various Boards and discuss the problems and any difficulties resulting from a possible merger. Likewise there was the exciting prospect of strengthening this essential arm of the Christian Kingdom by united action." Adopted was a six-point agenda of surveying and discussing the board organizations, the new problems of merger, and the strengthening of the trend toward merger.

The committee arrived at positive but general conclusions.

The survey quickly revealed the obvious fact that there are co-operative actions in indigenous churches across all Lutheran Synodical lines. These churches are at the point where there can be mergers more naturally and without the historic traditions and problems of the Western churches.

It is evident that discussion of mergers should look toward co-operation with other Lutheran groups not in present conversations.

Also, the Lutheran Foreign Missions Conference brings together all groups, and is of increasing importance as the Western church considers its mission in proclaiming the Gospel in other lands. Everything should be done to strengthen this co-operative conference.

It agreed that there were areas that required "interesting exploration insofar as relationships are concerned," as for instance the Santal Mission and the mission work in Hong Kong and Taiwan, but it also found that "there are no areas in which these four synods are at work in which there is any overlapping."

The committee then turned to personnel and organization, agreeing readily on "a common personnel pool." Present appointments and funding support from the churches were surveyed, and "it was agreed that the Board of the merged churches should be large enough in order that all fields might be adequately represented and all phases of merging churches represented." There was also "general agreement that due consideration must be made in the national benevolent budget of the church for the work and program of the merged Boards."

The spirit was upbeat. "There was enthusiastic agreement . . . that the work of world missions will be enormously strengthened by the merger of our churches. We see the possibility of uniting talents, resources, breaking provincial boundaries, deepening spiritual ties and giving encouragement to national churches by such a merger." But there was also acknowledgment of the new signs on the fields; not much, perhaps, but the mention of "indigenous churches," as quoted above, is an indication of developments to come. Attention was given to a number of practical problems, and it was noted that the ULCA was establishing a School of Missions at Chicago.

The JCLU took kindly to the reports of the committee, which continued its work. Already at a committee meeting on December 30, 1957, a complete "Outline of Organization and Function of Foreign Missions of the United Church" was adopted. It laid down the principles to be followed in the framing of the constitution and the by-laws of a Board of World Missions. The work and planning of the committee went on, as work and planning has gone on ever since. There is no field of church endeavor in which world developments and changes of attitudes have had as far-reaching and penetrating an influence as in the area of world missions. Circumstances have made it necessary to rethink radically the nature and methods of missions, and this has undoubtedly brought the profound nature of missions closer to the very core of the church and its work. It would be presumptuous, however, in a short survey to attempt a summary and diagnosis, and this report will therefore close with the provisions for World Missions in the by-laws of the LCA.

Section X, H.   Board of World Missions.

Item 1.   The objects of the board shall be:

   a. The proclamation of the Gospel in word and deed and the administration of the sacraments in behalf of this church outside the Dominion of Canada and the United States of America.

   b. Assistance and support of sister churches in the areas hereinafter named, where evangelical Christians are a small minority.

   c. Establishment of indigenous churches where they do not exist.

The areas mentioned were: Argentina, British Guiana, China, Hong Kong, India, Japan, Liberia, Malaya, Tanganyika, Uruguay.

            * * *

The specific organization of each board was a task to be taken care of by the boards themselves, guided by the by-laws and responsible to the Executive Council. A detailed description and analysis of each board with its varying characteristics would go beyond the concern of this presentation. Furthermore, the entire framework and pattern of the tasks undertaken by the boards and commissions were so altered by the restructuring a decade later that a discussion now would be academic. The concern of this chapter has not been to discuss contemporary problems or to blueprint the future; it has been, as has been stated elsewhere, to visualize what the JCLU was trying to do and why.

It might be said that the story of this section weaves together two strands of activity into a single cord for the use of the church, but the metaphor is not entirely apt. The two strands are placed in the same hand, but they are still two different, albeit related, lines of endeavor. The one has to do with the immediate concern of the Christian community for individuals who are ill, deprived, or underprivileged in some way or another. This activity expresses itself in the common establishment of institutions for the alleviation of human need: hospitals, children's homes, homes for the aged, and so on. It is an activity of love and is so called, but due to the condescending implications of charity as almsgiving, the noble word "charity," by which the English language has translated Paul's term *"agape,"* has come into disrepute, and another Greek expression, meaning the same but less susceptible to misinterpretation, has commonly and even euphemistically been used, namely, "eleemosynary" activity. All four churches had been supportive of such activity, often in cooperation with other churches or agencies, the record of Augustana probably being the most outstanding, relatively speaking. The abundance and proliferation of institutions of mercy posed a tangled problem of transfer and coordination, albeit a gratifying one.

The other strand was the activity that has been called social action. It relates to the larger community of the nation and mankind and it is expressed in statements rather than in direct action. Protests against social injustice, programs for human improvement, frameworks for action—these works of the mind and of the pen are often mighty and the four churches had given voice to them. The still small voices of the smaller churches, which were more effective in the creation of membership attitudes rather than in efficacious general action, were probably not widely noticed, but both Augustana and the ULCA had formidable records of program and protest. The coordination of these efforts in the new church posed less of a problem than the eleemosynary, for their nature was that of the common realm, and the progressive spirit that had prompted them found kinship in each other's company.

The Joint Commission took early action to initiate plans in these areas. On January 10, 1957, the Committee on Powers and Functions recorded:

> We agree that a plan should be devised whereby eleemosynary institutions shall be related to the constituent units. There shall be a Board of Social Missions of the General Body for purposes of counseling, setting of standards, coordination etc.

In regard to social action, the same committee took action on February 10, 1957.

> There shall be an administrative unit of the General Body concerned with matters in this field.

The tangled skein of interrelationships and even interownership of institutions of social welfare led the Commission to an early consideration of an inter-Lutheran solution to the problem. The Committee on Powers and Functions recommended in June 1957 and again in September 1957 that "the new church ask the National Lutheran Council to accept and assume major responsibility to act in its behalf in . . . counseling all inner mission agencies related to it, including those owned and controlled by its constituent units in addition to those which are inter-Lutheran in character." It further recommended that the members appointed by the new church to the National Lutheran Council's Division of Welfare should constitute a Commission on Inner Missions. Such plans obviously foundered when the merger of NLC's churches into two major bodies made it necessary to create a new kind of council on the national scene.

The Committee on Powers and Functions dominated the picture yet in February 1959 when it met as a committee to consider the reports of other committees which were yet to probe the possibilities of making arrangements with the National Lutheran Council and to make studies regarding the structure of a board with the possibility of combining the two concerns under one board. The result of the discussion was formulated in two agreements: "It was agreed that the proposal to have a Commission or Board of Social Missions to function in connection with the Division of Welfare of the National Lutheran Council was impractical and under certain conditions undesirable." "It was moved to recommend to the JCLU that in the area of Inner (Social) Missions and Social Action there shall be one board with two departments—the Department of Social Missions and the Department of Social Action." Having thus emerged from the intricacies involved in the desires and traditions of four churches and a common church agency, the Committee on Powers and Functions outlined the objectives and functions of the board and its two departments. In regard to the Department of Social Missions there were thirteen points, most of which had to do with practical procedures. The first four have general interest, however.

The functions of the Department of Social Missions shall be:

1. Develop and interpret a comprehensive social mission policy throughout the church that is applicable to synod and congregation as well as agency and institution.

2. Develop and maintain a helpful relationship with synodical social mission boards or committees, institutions and agencies and institutional chaplains.

3. Promote the spirit and program of Christian service in the synods and congregations.

4. Conduct conferences and workshops.

The Department of Social Action received ten points of instruction of which six are quoted here:

The functions of the Department of Social Action shall be [to]:

1. Initiate and direct objective studies and assemble the results of surveys and research relating to specific social problems to the end that the church may be provided with factual materials for its guidance in implementing its social concern.

2. Explore ways and means of combating social evils, influencing and crystalizing public opinion, securing proper social legislation, and awakening the social conscience of the community.

3. Formulate statements on social issues for the consideration of the church.

4. Prepare and edit educational materials to be released through the church.

5. Recruit, encourage, and assist in the training of leaders in social action.

6. Give counsel, instruction, and guidance on the position of the church in specific social issues. . . .

A Committee on Lutheran Health and Welfare Institutions and Agencies was then appointed, consisting of Harold Haas (chairman), Lawrence Holt, Holger P. Jorgensen, and Douglas Ollila. In a report in March 1959 the committee reveals the involved problems. "There are a large number of agencies. The Division of Welfare of the NLC lists the existence of several hundred health and welfare agencies and institutions in the U.S.A. and Canada." One of the four churches had 110 institutions plus 65 inter-Lutheran ones. The committee calls attention to the fact that policies vary considerably, that size and nature of services are different, and that 82 agencies have no other relationship to the church than the support and participation of individual members of congregations. The committee was given further instructions by the JCLU. "What we want as a JCLU is information about the institutions of an eleemosynary character, their present relationship and suggested possible relationship to constituent units of the new church."

After meeting on April 27–28, 1959, the committee responded that it "has had a great deal of difficulty in trying to fulfill its assignment. This is due to the nature of the situation in which the church finds itself relative to welfare institutions and agencies. . . . The Committee made several attempts to set up classification of relationships to the church. It was found that such a listing was deceptive rather than descriptive, so this was abandoned." It decided therefore to list all agencies according to the proposed synodical pattern, "where there is presently a relationship to one or more of the merging bodies" and where the new church should take them over. It also listed the agencies where there was no present genuine relationship, plus a list of information about ALC and Missouri agencies and other agencies receiving support. The report suggested directions and guidelines for coming relationships, too detailed to be reported here, but it placed the problems and responsibilities squarely before the JCLU.

After a meeting on September 8–9, 1961, the committee made a final report, which pointed out continuing problems.

> In spite of utilizing all the resources that were available to the committee, it is not possible to present to the JCLU a complete, carefully delineated, picture of Lutheran social mission agencies and institutions in their relationship to the future synods of the LCA. To pretend to do so would be false to the complexities of the actual situation. The solution of many of these complexities will depend on actions of synods that are not yet in existence.

It reiterated a philosophy stated earlier, "that Lutheran health and welfare agencies and institutions (those in which the church participates in any formal way) should be integral parts of the ministry and structure of the church," and it repeated the concern for agencies that were "severely disturbed by the fact of merger." It listed the institutions and agencies "presently related to jurisdictional units" of the four churches and added: "This is as close as we can come to a 'certified list' " that will be a part of the new church.

The approach to the administrative direction of social ministry in the new church was formulated by the Committee on Powers and Functions and the Committee on Constitutions. Their work was embodied in the constitution and by-laws of the LCA, which established a Board of Social Ministry with two departments, the Department of Social Missions and the Department of Social Action. It also established that the relationship of social agencies should be a synodical concern and that the LCA board should "encourage and stimulate the related synodical committees, offer them counsel and guidance, and . . . assist them with staff service and special grants for specific purposes." In regard to social action, "the Board of Social Ministry shall conduct research relating to moral issues in the life of society for the guidance of the church in expressing its social concern." Further, "the board shall, at its discretion, formulate statements on moral and social questions for consideration by conventions." It was furthermore suggested that the board should initiate programs and make arrangements for discussion institutes.

# 9. Evangelism, Stewardship, and Auxiliaries

The ecclesiastical catchwords of the years immediately following World War II, when ecumenical and international cooperation flowered and there was a great and penitent desire to bind up the wounds of war, were "evangelism" and "stewardship." The church had survived the holocaust, or the deluge, if you please, and it was concerned to demonstrate its will to serve. Muscles were to be flexed and the dynamics of the churches were to be demonstrated, for they had brought the ship of the church safely through the storms. This survival theme can be traced back to the story of the ark in Genesis, of course, and when it was used in the second century by the author of 1 Peter he said that the occupants of the ark were saved through water, which corresponds to baptism (1 Pet. 3:20–21), that is, through incorporation into the life of God. This was not the postwar theme of the churches, however. The church, and perhaps even the world, was to be saved through the efforts of Christian responsibility and helpfulness, namely, evangelism and stewardship.

Evangelism and stewardship, rightly understood and rightly placed in context, are central and significant. Evangelism is the proclamation of the gospel, and stewardship is responsible activity on behalf of the gospel, a "manner of life . . . worthy of the gospel" (Phil. 1:27). As they were promoted in the postwar years, however, and even as they are understood today, evangelism and stewardship are often identified with institutional functions of promotion and support. There is nothing wrong with institutional promotion and support, of course. The church as an institution in society cannot exist in a modern world without efficacious efforts in this direction, and these should therefore be honored. The problem is that an identification is permitted and perpetuated and that an impression is given that institutional promotion and support are one and the same as the primary expressions of the Christian spirit. In the 1970s we are beginning, under the scourge of more recent events and developments, to see the fallacy of this, to wit, the theological affirmation effort of the LCA and the basics of "Strength for Mission." We must therefore today place a question mark behind the exuberant and optimistic efforts of the 1950s, but let not this be a criticism of the genuine character and serious intent of the effort to face a crucial situation twenty years ago.

All four churches of the merger had been involved in efforts of evangelism and stewardship, and there was no question that there were to be programs of this nature in the new church. This was expressed in resolutions by the Committee on Powers and Functions on February 15, 1957.

> An administrative unit of the general body shall be responsible for the program, planning and coordination in the field of evangelism. . . . The implementation of evangelism will be the responsibility of the constituent units, singly and in groups.

> An administrative unit of the general body shall be responsible for the program, planning and coordination in the field of stewardship. . . . Special attention is called to the existence of the Lutheran Laymen's Movement in the ULC and the possibility of incorporating and expanding this movement in the new church. . . . The implementation of stewardship will be the responsibility of the constituent units.

The groundwork was thus laid, but the actual planning of institutional efforts was not undertaken until the basic structures of the new church had been determined and the constitution had received its first approval in the summer of 1960.

Upon the recommendation of the Steering Committee, the JCLU adopted the following directive at its September 1961 meeting:

> That the Sub-Committee on the Commission on Evangelism be instructed to confer with the departmental committee of the Department of Evangelism of the Board of Social Missions of the ULCA and the Committee on Evangelism of the Board of American Missions of the Augustana Lutheran Church, and individuals to be designated by the presidents of AELC and the Suomi Synod, using this group as consultants for the development of a recommended program for the Commission.

The Committee on Evangelism met December 15–16, 1961, with the following members: Alfred Stone (chairman), J. Sabin Swanson, Peter D. Thomsen, and Oliver Hallberg. Official consultants were

William Berg and J. Bruce Weaver. Also present as consultants were nine persons from Augustana, five from the ULCA, and one from Suomi. The committee set itself the goal of defining the program, determining the staff, and developing the budget of a proposed Commission on Evangelism of the LCA.

The work of the Committee on Evangelism was done in three areas. The first area was a reporting and exploration of the evangelism work of the four merging churches. These presentations are referred to in the minutes of the committee but they are not detailed. The third area was that of planning the organization of evangelism work in regard to personnel and funding, and this phase is reported but seems too technical to record. In between these two agenda items of the December 1961 meeting is sandwiched a discussion of the nature and program of evangelism. There is mention of an "Exhibit I" called "Projected Program of Evangelism in the LCA." This would be an important source of information about the thinking of the committee. Unfortunately, however, repeated searches in the archive deposits have not unearthed this exhibit. For some reason it is not included in the appendixes to the JCLU minutes and it has not been discovered in any other deposit of material. Inquiries of half a dozen members of the committee have not brought this sixteen-year-old document to light. Readers will therefore have to content themselves by proceeding directly to the end result of the planning by the committee. This is found in the by-laws, which undoubtedly reflect the committee proposals. The key provisions are therefore quoted:

BY-LAWS, Section XI, D.  Commission on Evangelism.

Item 1.  The commission shall consist of twenty members.

Item 2.  The commission shall give leadership for this church in evangelism through creative thinking, development of plans and recommended programs, preparation of printed and other materials, the holding of church-wide and regional training conferences, and such supplementary service by its staff as it finds to be possible and the synods desire.

Item 3.  To give effect to the principle that the quickening of congregational evangelism is primarily the concern of synods in the structure of this church, each synod shall have a committee on evangelism to direct the synodical evangelism staff if any, and in general fulfill the basic responsibility resting on the synod in this phase of its ministry to congregations.

Item 4. The commission shall encourage and stimulate its related synodical committees and shall assist them with counsel and guidance. . . .

Item 5. The commission shall plan, structure, administer and supervise such special, church-wide concerted efforts in evangelism as this church may authorize and undertake from time to time.

Item 6. Associate secretaries of the commission may be assigned to live and work in specified geographical areas. . . .

* * *

After the resolution of February 15, 1957, mentioned above, the Committee on Powers and Functions next considered the matter of stewardship at a meeting on November 2, 1957, and the following motion, made by Franklin Clark Fry, was adopted:

1. There shall be a department of stewardship, operating under the authority and responsibility of the executive group of the general church body, functioning through staff appointed by the executive group.

2. The Lutheran Laymen's Movement for Stewardship shall be continued and expanded in general in its present type of organization and functioning.

A. This pattern of organization includes:

(1) Membership by individuals on a voluntary basis, involving annual contributions and commitment to stewardship activity.

(2) Election of an executive body by the conventions of the general body or its executive group.

(3) Accountability to the conventions of the church and in the interim to its executive group.

B. Present functions include:

(1) Preparation and dissemination of stewardship.

(2) Stewardship films and visual aids.

(3) A fund-raising counseling service.

3. All common concerns of the department and the Lutheran Laymen's Movement for Stewardship, including nomination of staff members, determination of salaries and policies, etc., shall be cleared through a counseling committee representative of both of them and appointed by the executive group.

4. A common investing Fund shall be available for the investment of permanent capital funds of the general body, its constituent units,

boards, congregations, institutions, etc.  It shall be operated under the authority and direction of the executive group, aided by a board of directors of the C.I.F. elected by the executive group.

Both the resolutions of the Committee on Powers and Functions point up the problem of reconciling practices of stewardship, Augustana and the ULCA having different methods.  In Augustana stewardship was a direct concern of the church; in the ULCA stewardship had been in the hands of the Lutheran Laymen's Movement, which was a most highly esteemed organization, difficult to give up.  Could the two approaches be reconciled?

The documentation of what happened concerning this issue is not only complicated but elusive; one needs the thread of Ariadne to emerge from the maze.  Documentation is not available and perhaps not necessary.  From conversation with individuals who participated in the running debate between advocates of two systems, it is known that long and fervent discussions took place.  Eventually the compromise plan that was to be the end result was shaped.  It is reflected in the report issued to the four churches in the summer of 1958, which contained the following paragraph on stewardship.

There is to be a Commission on Stewardship, operating under the authority and responsibility of the Executive Council, functioning through staff appointed by the Executive Council.

The Lutheran Laymen's Movement for Stewardship (of the ULCA) is to be continued and expanded in general in its present type of organization and functioning.  This pattern includes:

a. Membership by individuals on a voluntary basis, involving annual contributions and commitment to stewardship activity.

b. Election of an executive body by the conventions of the general body or its executive council.

c. Accountability to the conventions of the church and in the interim to the executive council.

Present functions of the LLM include:

a. Preparation and dissemination of stewardship literature.

b. Stewardship films and visual aids.

c. A fund-raising counseling service.

All common concerns of the Commission and of the Lutheran Laymen's Movement for Stewardship, including nomination of staff members, determination of salaries and policies, etc., are to be cleared through a consulting committee representative of both of them and appointed by the executive council.

After the lull around the first adoption by the churches of the constitution for the new church during the summer of 1960, planning work was resumed on stewardship. A report to the JCLU of a committee meeting held on January 18–19, 1962, tells the story.

A joint meeting of stewardship leaders of the four merging churches was held in Chicago, November 8-9, 1961 to carry out the purpose laid down by the JCLU: "to develop and set in motion a unified program of Stewardship promotion to be carried on in 1962 in preparation for the Every Member Visitation of that year for the securing of funds of the 1963 Budget of the LCA, with the understanding that the chief staff officer of the future Commission on Stewardship, when nominated in the early months of 1962, will assume the leadership of this undertaking from that time forward." (September, 1961, Steering Committee Minutes).

The Joint Committee on Stewardship was organized and is made up of the seven members of the Augustana Committee on Stewardship Education, the six members of the ULCA Stewardship Department Consulting Committee, and one representative each from the AELC and Suomi. LeRoy Breneman, ULCA, was elected chairman and Carl H. Hansen, Augustana, secretary. The convener of the meeting was Dr. Martin Carlson, acting as deputy for the chairman of JCLU.

The committee members were: (ULCA) Eugene S. Heckathorn, Alfred L. Beck, LeRoy Breneman, Walter H. Hagey, Everett G. Mitchell, and Clarence Stoughton; (Augustana) Everett Norling, Melville Sjostrand, Carl Hansen, Carl W. Segerhammer, Al Wellens, Rodney Davis, and Earl Anderson; (AELC) Harry C. Jensen; (Suomi) W. G. Ruohomaki. The content of this meeting and a subsequent one held on February 22–23, 1962, concerned itself with practical details of stewardship planning, and the final decisions concerning organization and purpose are contained in the by-laws of the new church.

BY-LAWS, Section XI, F. Commission on Stewardship.

Item 1. The commission shall consist of twenty members, of whom five shall be ministers and fifteen shall be laymen.

Item 2. The underlying pervasive purpose of the commission shall be to arouse and lead the members of the congregations of this church to practice their Christian faith in all aspects of their daily lives. An immediate objective shall be to encourage Christian giving through offerings for the Lutheran Church in America and its congregations and synods.

Item 3. The commission shall develop the basic stewardship program and procedures for the Lutheran Church in America for approval by the convention or the Executive Council.

Item 4. Each synod shall have a committee on stewardship to direct the synodical stewardship staff, if any, and in general fulfill the primary responsibility resting upon the synod in this phase of its ministry to its congregations.

Item 5. The commission shall encourage and stimulate its related synodical committees, giving counsel, guidance and, as desired by them and to the degree of its own ability, assistance through field service. With the consent of the synodical committee that is concerned, the commission may conduct experimental or pilot programs within one or more of the congregations of a synod.

Item 6. By virtue of their appointment to this commission, its lay members shall simultaneously constitute the executive committee of the Lutheran Laymen's Movement for Stewardship, with the ministerial members serving in an advisory capacity. The work of the commission and of said executive committee in stewardship education and promotion shall be completely unified. They shall have a single integrated staff for such activities, serving under this commission and nominated by the Commission on Stewardship to the Executive Council for election. The executive committee of the Lutheran Laymen's Movement for Stewardship shall act separately only for the purpose of caring for the movement's own business, including cultivation of its membership, and to supervise specific projects or undertakings for which the convention of the Executive Council has made the movement responsible.

Item 7. Members of the Lutheran Laymen's Movement for Stewardship shall have the right to submit nominations in writing for consideration by the Executive Council in appointing this commission.

Parallel to this comprehensive coverage the Lutheran Laymen's Movement received its recognition, and again the by-laws demonstrate the thinking.

BY-LAWS, Section XIII. Lutheran Laymen's Movement for Stewardship.

Item 1. The Lutheran Laymen's Movement for Stewardship, a voluntary fellowship of individuals devoted to the cultivation of ideals of Christian stewardship and to the evocation of a worthy response in the Lutheran Church in America, shall be recognized as having the status of being in association with this church.

Item 2. In addition to the lay members of its executive committee, the membership of the movement shall consist of laymen of this church who make annual contributions as specified in by-laws approved by the Executive Council and who commit themselves to personal efforts for stewardship in their congregations and in support of the movement as a whole.

Item 3. Everything that the movement does in the field of direct stewardship education and promotion shall be done through and under the direction of the Commission on Stewardship.

Item 4. The internal affairs of the movement and any collateral activities assigned to it by the convention or the Executive Council shall be carried on in conformity with the applicable established policies of this church, and full report of all operations shall be made to the convention and upon request to the Executive Council.

* * *

The "auxiliary," the name for a functional group within the institutional church, is certainly an American phenomenon if not an American creation. As an adjective the term means "supplemental," and the suggestion of its use is that the worshiping community is in need of supplemental activity and organization. Traditionally most American churches have such supplemental activity, but it would carry this presentation too far to try to document its origin and development. Suffice it to say that the four churches uniting through the Joint Commission had official or semi-official activities which could, with a general name, be called auxiliaries. It was therefore taken for granted in the Commission that there should be auxiliaries in the new church in the traditional categories of women's work, men's work, and youth work. The Committee on Powers and Functions put this into official language on February 15, 1957, when it stated that "the new church should have three recognized auxiliaries related to the general body. . . . Such auxiliaries shall be responsible and subject to the decisions of the conventions of the general body, and in the interim shall receive and be guided by counsel from the officers of the church. . . . The auxiliaries responsible to constituent units will need further study."

The Committee on Auxiliaries had the following members: Carl J. Tamminen, Oscar W. Carlson, Enok Mortensen, and Leonard Kendall. It met on September 29, 1958, and prepared a report containing "Presuppositions" and "General Principles," directions for organizing on the congregational level, the synodical level, and the General Church level, plus a set of "Specific Principles." The report was discussed and tentatively received by the Commission; it was revised on February 9, 1959, approved with recommendations by the Commission in March 1959, and then put into final shape. The "Presuppositions" and "General Principles" of this document are worth noting.

PRESUPPOSITIONS:

1. The auxiliaries are an outgrowth of the sense of Christian vocation and the Scriptural concept of stewardship, and the desire for Christian fellowship.

2. They are also a product of the natural desire for people of like church-related interests to band together for the purpose of advancing those interests.

3. In the history of the Church the auxiliaries have performed a useful function and have justified their existence and continuance, and therefore the merged Church ought to sponsor the establishment of auxiliaries.

4. Auxiliaries ought to exist for the purpose of service to the congregations, and these purposes must be consistent with the congregations' purposes.

5. Individual personal responsibility to the congregation is always primary; the auxiliary should amplify and provide service to the congregation by means of personal expression and participation.

GENERAL PRINCIPLES:

1. Provision shall be made by the merged church for auxiliaries.

2. The auxiliaries are basically auxiliaries of the congregation to which they give allegiance and service.

3. The auxiliaries shall exist for the general purpose of:
   —Development of a sense of Christian vocation.
   —Providing resources for the expression of Christian responsibility.
   —Cultivation of spiritual attitudes and motives.
   —Education in the life and work of the church.
   —Providing avenues of service and closer fellowship.
   —Stimulation of the Christian life in home and community.
   —Sponsorship of such causes as are assigned by the church.

4. The church should provide a medium of inclusive and continuing coordination between the auxiliaries and the Church's boards and agencies which serve congregational life.

It was the suggestion of the committee that "the General Church for

the present shall have only three official auxiliaries: one each for . . .
men, . . . women, . . . youth." Under "Specific Principles" the committee suggested the following as objects and purposes of all
auxiliaries:

> In coordination with the authority of Boards and Agencies all auxili-
> aries may serve in the areas of:
>
> —Missions
> —Evangelism
> —Works of Mercy
> —Stewardship
> —The Christian Home and the Community
> —Education
> —Social Action
> —Recreation
> —Leadership Development
> —Vocational Guidance

The groundwork performed by the committee for the general
planning of auxiliaries was incorporated by the Commission into the
constitutional documents in three ways. Article XVII of the constitution laid the foundation by stating briefly:

> Section 1. General organizations of men, women, and youth of this
> church formed to further and support its work and for Christian edifi-
> cation and fellowship, may be recognized as official auxiliaries of the
> Lutheran Church in America by vote of the convention. Auxiliaries
> possess autonomy except as stipulated in this constitution, the by-laws,
> or actions of the convention applying thereto.
>
> Section 2. The president of this church or his representative shall
> have a seat and voice on the convention of the auxiliaries and in their
> executive bodies.
>
> Section 3. Each auxiliary may appoint an advisory member to each
> board and commission.
>
> Section 4. Each auxiliary shall make report of its work to the regular
> conventions of this church.

The by-laws, Section XIV, dealt with "Church-wide Agencies and
Auxiliaries in General." It provided for the organization, responsibilities, and procedures of such bodies and stated as an introduction:

> Item 1. The constitution and by-laws, and amendments thereto, of
> the boards and auxiliaries shall go into effect after approval by the
> convention or the Executive Council.

Finally, the by-laws stated the principles of auxiliaries. These were, for the most part, a condensed reproduction of the "General Principles" of the committee, but one addition was made. In response to a concern that the purposes of the auxiliaries were weighted too much toward "service" or "services," a first point ("a") was added, particularly upon the initiative of the AELC delegation.

BY-LAWS, Section XIV, A.   Principles of Organization.

Item 1.   The auxiliaries shall exist for the general purpose of:

   a. Mutual expression of Christian living.
   b. Cultivation of the spiritual life and of evangelical attitudes and motives.
   c. Development of a sense of Christian vocation.
   d. Providing a vehicle for the expression of individual Christian responsibility.
   e. Education in the life and work of the Church, and in particular of the Lutheran Church in America.
   f. Opening up avenues of service and fellowship.
   g. Stimulation of Christian living in home and community.
   h. Sponsorship of such causes as are assigned to them by this church.

After the first adoption of the new constitution by the church conventions of the summer of 1960, the work of planning three auxiliaries was taken up full force. These discussions, reports, proposals, and final adoptions are far too extensive to be included here. Furthermore, some of this work is now part of the past. The men's auxiliary and the youth auxiliary were either absorbed in the changes resulting from the restructuring or were diverted into other channels. The women's auxiliary, Lutheran Church Women, continues to serve as it was planned and constituted.

# 10. Communication

For the Christian church, communication takes place primarily in worship; the proclamation of the gospel is the essential communication. The professed word and the corresponding participation in Christ through the sacrament is the heart of the gospel. "Make disciples of all nations by baptizing" is the essence of the great injunction; not make disciples and then baptize. Immediately following this, however, the injunction stresses teaching, the next step in communication. There is all the difference in the world between communication by proclamation and sacramental participation on the one hand and communication by teaching on the other, but that does not mean that teaching is not of utmost importance. The church teaches by informing and explaining. It tells the story recorded in Scripture and history and explains what this means. The church informs and illuminates its members about the privileges and tasks of living today.

The four churches of the merger were, as a matter of course, vitally engaged in communication through teaching programs, expressed in preparation and performance, and through church papers. Augustana, the ULCA, and Suomi also had publishing houses— Augustana Book Concern, Muhlenberg Press, the Finnish Book Concern—and the problem confronting the JCLU was therefore not the establishment of new ways and precedents but rather the choice between a variety and the concentration upon effectiveness and quality. The planning fell into three categories to be considered in the following: parish education, church papers, and the publication enterprise.

## Parish Education

A Committee on Parish Education met three times in the summer of 1957. The exact membership of the committee is not immediately discernible from the records, for fourteen names are given with committee members and consultants listed indiscriminately.  In the last report of the committee, however, dated January 3, 1962, the following are listed as members: Walter B. Freed (chairman), Howard Christensen, Frank Efird, L. Boyd Hamm, Martin J. Heinecken, David F. Engstrom, Robert Hetico, and Martin L. Raymond.  Consultants were W. Kent Gilbert, S. White Rhyne, and Lael H. Westberg, with Gilbert acting as secretary.  The work of the committee was immeasurably favored by the fact that the same people had been engaged for some time in the Long-Range Program for Parish Education.  This committee had already agreed upon a statement of purpose, which the JCLU committee adopted as its own:

Inasmuch as the church, as the body of Christ, seeks to become more effectively that community of believers in which the Holy Spirit calls, gathers, enlightens, and sanctifies individuals in their relationships with God and their fellow men, the church's central educational objective, therefore, shall be—

To assist the individual in his response and witness to the eternal and incarnate Word of God as he grows in this community of the church toward greater maturity in his Christian life through ever-deepening understandings, more wholesome attitudes, and more responsible patterns of action.

The committee also made recommendations for the basic responsibilities of a Board of Parish Education in the new church, to wit:

The Board of Parish Education should have full responsibility for outlining, developing, and promoting a total program of parish education for the United States, including:

1. All schools and agencies of parish education recommended for all age levels in the congregations, such as the home, the Sunday church school, the vacation church school, the weekday church school, the catechetical classes (youth and adult), special interest groups, summer camps and conferences, and such other agencies as tend to strengthen the program of Christian education in the parish.

2. All materials to be used in the field of parish education to implement the program.

3. The means of developing leadership for this program.

4. The promotion of the program in the congregations, constituent units, and the United Church through materials and field work.

The recommendation included the proposal that the Board of Parish Education continue to develop a Long-Range Program for Parish Education. The remainder of this first report, submitted to the JCLU in September 1957, concerned itself with a multitude of practical matters such as membership on the board, organizational functions, and funding. Most of these suggestions were incorporated into the by-laws proposed in 1960 and finally adopted in 1962 (Section X, C). Three meetings were held in the fall of 1961 to review current concerns and to prepare budget and practices for the board of the church-to-be.

## Church Papers

The matter of church papers was routine and prejudged. There was to be one official paper and by the weight of prestige and circulation this was to be the ULCA paper *The Lutheran*. The reasons for this are easy to surmise but difficult to document; the end result is the best documentation. The argument was primarily that of circulation, that is, financial, but the outcome was monopolistic, even monolithic. This is not said to disparage the policy or the quality of *The Lutheran* under the able and experienced editorship of G. Elson Ruff, who was the preeminent and undisputed choice to be at the helm. It is a little difficult to understand in retrospect, however, why only one journal was chosen. The journalistic and philosophic traditions of the other three churches were also distinguished and had qualities of their own to add to the public expression of the new church. As it turned out, they were eliminated—unless they were non-English, thus turning ethnic heritages back to a nineteenth-century status of a "foreign language" category.

With the end result predetermined, the task of the Committee on Church Papers, appointed in December 1957, was routine, and the committee, consisting of Joseph Sittler (chairman), Thorvald Hansen (secretary), O. V. Anderson, and Ahti Karjala, performed their work with dispatch and competence. There should, therefore, not be much of interest to report. When, nevertheless, the fatigued researcher who has safaried through endless reams of identical reports with their points and subpoints and "whereases" comes across the report of the Committee on Church Papers, he knows that he has come to an oasis of style and interest. The report of March 1957 is not signed, but there can be no doubt that the style is that of Dr. Sittler:

> The nature of the principal authorized periodical of this Church is determined by the basic problems of education, nurture, and information which are intrinsic to the merging process itself. This periodical should confront the Church with a vision of its common task and opportunity. It will be necessary, during the consolidation and acquaintance-deepening period of this Church's life that there be a periodical for the service of the common life and at the average level of the people.
>
> This committee had been charged with policy decisions which it feels it can make most intelligently only on the basis of professional studies intended to disclose: (1) who reads our present periodicals, (2) what content evokes a positive response, (3) what areas of common concern ought be more fully cultivated, etc. We ask, therefore, that JCLU consider making financial provision for professional gathering and analysis of such information. The assessment of such data and the translation of its significance into specific plans will, of course, be a continuing duty of a church paper's committee.
>
> In anticipation of such a survey and the subsequent interpretation and implementation of its findings, the Church ought, we believe, call to its help from among its membership men of specialized competence in varied fields related to the project. We therefore ask permission to arrange for ad hoc consultative conferences.
>
> The committee believes that the principal authorized periodical must address the whole Church, and reflect the mind and spirit of the whole Church. While the promotion of the programs of the Church is an essential function of such a periodical, its purpose and scope transcend such promotional activity. The report previously submitted and amended by JCLU, adequately provides for editorial integrity and responsibility.
>
> The committee believes that it may be feasible during the interim before merger to solve a measure of coordination among our existing periodicals.
>
> Although the main concern of this committee has been the study of an effective periodical for the common life and average level of our people, we believe it is necessary also to plan for a reflective journal of opinion and discussion aimed at the clergy and concerned laity of the Church. Your committee awaits a decision on this proposal.

After this essay the end result is prosaic, but let the by-laws speak:

BY-LAWS, Section XIII—Periodicals.

Item 1. "The Lutheran" shall be a magazine designed to appeal to and hold the interest of the whole constituency of the church.

Item 2. Official notices of this church, and of the dates and places of conventions of the synods, shall be published in "The Lutheran."

## Publication

The initiative was again taken by the Committee on Powers and Functions, the first time on June 10, 1957:

> We agree that the Powers and Functions of publication and printing of the official organization shall be the prerogative of the general body. The constituent units shall have the privilege of printing their own minutes and news sheets.

This was spelled out more in detail on June 24, 1957.

It is recommended:

A. The publication activities of the new church be defined in general as the responsibility of the General Body.

B. The constituent units be assured the right to publish their own official documents, minutes and news sheets.

C. A sub committee be appointed by the chairman of JCLU upon nomination of the church body presidents to arrive at a more specific formulation.

The committee consisted of the heads of the publishing agencies, Birger Swenson of the Augustana Book Concern, H. Torrey Walker of Muhlenberg Press, Ahti Karjala of Suomi, and Thorvald Hansen of the AELC. Swenson was elected chairman. The committee met for the first time on October 29, 1957. It was immediately apparent that the matter of coordinating or even merging as extensive and complex enterprises as publication houses was beyond the competence of premerger committees. This was expressed in three "assumptions" recorded by the first meeting:

ASSUMPTIONS

1. Because the Boards of Publication perform identical functions in their respective bodies, the essential elements in any merger are the determination of the basic structures of the governing body, arrangements for the administrative supervision of operations and a proposed charter or constitution.

2. Since the matters of detailed operation of production facilities, adjustment to a common accounting system and the establishment of uniform methods and procedures will require careful study and conference by staff members before submittal to a merged board, it is believed that no formula for these should be sought in advance of a merger.

3. That there are some questions which will only be answered when policies for the merged church have been developed and hence while this committee may state its opinions on these, it does so with the full understanding that there are other factors affecting the ultimate decision.

The committee made recommendations for a Board of Publication with twenty-one members, for stated officers, and for standing committees. The number and names of the proposed committees reflect the scope and involvement of the whole publication enterprise. They are: Manufacturing, Property and Real Estate, Literature, Ecclesiastical Arts, Periodicals, Audio-Visual Materials, Marketing, Promotion, and Public Relations. The committee was reluctant to go too much into details. "It is always difficult to find proper nomenclature for the staff of a Board of Publication because of all the boards of the church it has business connections not present in the program of other boards." Yet the committee saw "the advantages gained by using the same position names as other boards." That there was as yet no serious talk of the merger of agencies is reflected in the suggestion "that the plan for the administrative staff of the Board of Publication should provide for an Executive Secretary and three Associate Executive Secretaries (since there will be three bases of operation)."

The committee foresaw that the Board of Publication would be involved in two other functions of the new church: parish education and the church paper.

In providing for editorial staff two assumptions are made: (a) that the editorial work on curriculum will be the function of the staff of a Board of Parish Education and (b) that before planning for the editorial staff for church papers, certain decisions will have been made relative to responsibility for editorial content and policies of the papers and the papers which will be published.

It is assumed that a Board of Publication would have the responsibility for the publication and circulation of a church paper or papers since that has been the pattern in the four bodies discussing merger.

Finally, the committee recommended that "a detailed study of the publication work of the four bodies considering merger be prepared."

During the next four years the committee followed the work of the JCLU and gave counsel to developments. It "met regularly three times a year." At a meeting on September 25, 1961, it referred to the documents it had prepared in consultation with the JCLU. "These consist of a Joint Proposal of Merger, Articles of Merger and Proposed By-Laws." It also presented a Plan of Operation, the highlights of which were:

Provision for the continuance of the present distribution centers, 17 in all. . . .

The plans for the printing plants which are proposed are that Philadelphia and Rock Island each be equipped so that each plant can specialize in certain types of work. The plant in Hancock, Michigan, would continue to operate as it is now operating.

Paramentic vestments and church furnishings, it is suggested would be manufactured in Philadelphia as at present.

The practical arrangements of the Board of Publication were taken care of after the merger; they were too complicated and specific to be JCLU matters. The work of the JCLU was to decide and to put into constitutional paragraphs the foundational matters. This was done in the by-laws, parts of which are here quoted and parts of which are paraphrased.

BY-LAWS, Section E. Board of Publication.

Item 1. The Board of Publication shall be the publishing agency of the church. The dominant purpose of the board shall be the propagation of the Gospel and the edification of Christian believers through the printed word and through allied activities.

Item 2. The board shall print, or arrange for the printing of, the minutes of the conventions of the Lutheran Church in America and its year books. The board shall also publish the curricular materials produced by the Board of Parish Education and shall act in conjunction with the Commission on Church Papers as specified in Section XI, subsection C, of these by-laws, in the publication of the periodical of this church.

Item 3. [The board shall produce and distribute audio-visual materials and equipment and religious supplies.]

Item 4. The board shall carry on business operations. . . .

Item 5.  [Synods shall have the right to publish their documents. Other agencies shall be free to use the facilities of the board.]

Item 6.  [Available surpluses shall go to the church treasury.]

Item 7.  [Royalties payable to LCA for work done by boards shall be computed on formulas approved by the Executive Council.]

# 11. Budget, Finance, and Pensions

The Committee on Finance began its work after the Committee on Constitutions had presented its first drafts of the establishment of the new church. Part of its assignment was to review Section XVIII of the by-laws, which dealt with financial matters. The committee consisted of Martin E. Carlson (chairman), M. C. Miller (secretary), Edmund F. Wagner, and V. Richard Hietikko. It met for the first time on June 22, 1959, and continued a series of competent, critical, and valuable meetings until May 1962. Besides its immediate input into the structuring of the basic financial approach of the new church in its yearly budget, it made significant recommendations in the areas of corporate bank accounts, investment funds, and foundations—areas that baffle the average layman and, of course, the ecclesiastical historian. According to the massive sheaves of reports on file, it is evident that a major contribution was the planning of the first budget of the new church.

At its first meeting the committee undertook to examine the proposed financial setup in the constitutional documents prepared by the Committee on Constitutions. It accepted the basics of the proposals, often with the designation "full agreement," but it made valuable suggestions, most of which were eventually incorporated into the by-laws. A significant statement in its July 1959 report reflects the sound approach of the committee.

> The committee . . . agreed that its task was not necessarily to discover some common ground in the varied present patterns of operation in our several church bodies or merely to attempt a coordination of the same, but, recognizing that a new church is in the process of being erected, that the best possible fiscal structure should be devised for its operation. The committee did not feel under obligation to preserve everything possible of the present practices of one or more of the bodies. On the other hand, the committee had felt that it was free to recommend items which are not in the practices of any of the present bodies if such would be to the best interest of the new church.

It had some wise remarks concerning the budget.

> The committee recommends that the following principles be recognized in budgeting.
> 1. The budget is the fiscal statement of the program of the church. As such it must reflect the total program of the church and its beneficiary agencies and not only that part of a given program which is directly supported by the church. The budget should reflect the total work of the beneficiary agencies, including their support from all sources.
> 2. When budgets are adopted by the church they become the authorization for the program of the respective boards, commissions, or other activating groups.
> 3. Budgets should recognize the desire of individuals who would make gifts for specific purposes within the framework of the approved program of the church.

It also had a word of caution to the synods.

> The principle that synods shall incorporate the church apportionment together with the budget requirements for their own program needs and that the total of this shall constitute the annual synodical budget is sound. The principle that congregational contributions shall be divided proportionally, church and synod, is also sound. However, the committee recognized a possible problem here for which it does not at this point have a solution. There is nothing presently to prevent a synod from building an excessive budget for its own work with the result that if contributions are divided on a church-synod ratio as established by the budget the real program needs of the synod might be met while at the same time there would be a failure to meet the basic requirements of church program.

And the committee recommended a reserve to be set aside each year in order to provide for working capital for the coming year. It also recommended the establishment of a common investment fund and a foundation for the purpose of soliciting gifts.

The subsequent meetings were taken up with a great number of details concerning investments, property management, the setup of the fiscal office and fiscal policies, and budget policies and procedures. The committee followed closely the development of the by-laws. When the first LCA budget became an urgent matter in the fall of 1961, the committee worked closely with the presidents of the four churches to plan ahead. The chairman, Martin E. Carlson, exercising "whatever prerogatives might go with the committee chairmanship," made useful personal observations. In September 1961 the committee made the following observation:

It would seem imperative at this juncture that there be a general understanding among the merging bodies to the effect that no new work (expansion of the present program) which would involve commitments beyond January 1, 1963 be undertaken by any agency of present bodies without the consent of the corresponding agencies of the other three.

In December 1959 the Committee on Finance started to supplement its membership with representatives of the stewardship offices of the merging churches, plus representatives of conferences and synods, and in September 1961 the chairman called attention to the importance of interpretation.

One area in which JCLU might well give careful study and recommendation is that of responsibility for interpreting to the constituency the program and mission of the church. I mention it in this report because the decision will affect budgeting. Decisions are necessary for the Lutheran Church in America since the present merging bodies do not bring into the new church exactly comparable patterns of operation. . . . Furthermore, the Constitution and By-Laws do not seem to locate responsibility for this unless Section XI, F, Item 3 of the By-Laws which reads: "The commission [on Stewardship] shall develop the basic stewardship program and procedures for the LCA . . ." was intended to do this. No reference is made to this in the general outline of responsibility of individual boards.

It would appear that there are basically three possible approaches to this task:

1. Each agency of the church may have its own department of promotion and interpretation with the stewardship office being essentially a promotion and fund raising agency for the general budget.

2. Each agency of the church may have its own department of promotion and interpretation with one agency, such as a stewardship office, having responsibility to coordinate this activity.

3. One agency, such as the commission on stewardship, might be given entire responsibility for promotion and interpretation of the program and mission of the church with, of course, the privilege of drawing on information resources from every agency of the church and working in close consultation with them.

This is not the place to present the case for any particular approach to the problem. Since it is related, however, to our basic philosophy of the structure of the church and the nature of its mission, I would hope that JCLU would provide for a thorough study of the matter before arriving at a conclusion.

As far as a lay observer is concerned, most of the recommendations of the Committee on Finance were incorporated into the by-laws of the LCA, but not all the problems it raised were resolved. The description of the financial arrangements and procedures of the church are far too vast and complicated to be described here, however, and the reader is referred to Section XVIII of the by-laws.

*    *    *

It is an important characteristic of American church life, unknown and understood only with difficulty by European church people, where the national government provides for pensions, that church organizations have been compelled by practical circumstances to provide for retirement or disability benefits, particularly in a past when Social Security was not even dreamed of. This task has not been easy and it has never been met adequately. Larger church bodies have had fewer difficulties complying with actuarial practices, but for smaller churches it has been almost impossible to maintain a self-functioning system. They have therefore been forced to make pensions a direct budgetary concern, hoping to build endowments and to collect sufficient funds from contributions to hold budget lines down to a minimum. The actual pensions paid to retired pastors has therefore usually fallen short of an adequate retirement income and even short of the potential of larger church bodies. Suomi and the AELC were in the situation where they did not have a reserve pension plan, while Augustana and the ULCA had a "money-purchase plan on a sound actuarial basis." The question before the JCLU was how to coordinate and reconcile the two situations and to build a sound and workable plan for the future. This problem reversed the old saying that there are things that go beyond the mind of the ordinary person and into that of the preacher, for this problem went far beyond any theological acumen and into the realm of actuarial experts. Fortunately such experts were available, and they became servants of a compassionate concern for men and women who had given lifelong service in a calling not usually salaried in proportion to competence, dedication, and length of service.

In the JCLU the initiative was taken by the Committee on Powers and Functions on January 10, 1957, with a matter-of-course introduction: "We agree that the Function and Power of administrating pensions shall be the prerogative of the general body." In March 1957 the JCLU passed a motion "to establish a pension committee . . . to draft a broad outline of the pension arrangements, both organizational and financial, of the united church." This committee worked out not only the broad outline; it stuck with the task until every small detail of an enormously complicated organization had been arranged and presented to the new church. The Committee on Pensions, which accomplished this herculean task with admirable efficiency, consisted of George Hansen (AELC), Armas Holmio (Suomi), O. V. Anderson (Augustana), and James F. Henninger (ULCA). They were expertly assisted by L. Edwin Wang, executive secretary of Augustana Pension and Aid Fund, Robert Myers, chief actuary of the Social Security Administration and a member of the Board of Pensions of the ULCA, and George H. Berkheimer, executive secretary of the Board of Pensions, ULCA. The committee met for the first of many sessions on July 24, 1957; O. V. Anderson was elected chairman and George Berkheimer secretary.

The first meetings of the committee were necessarily explorative with a mutual sharing of information and exposing of problems. A resolution of mutual concern was passed that the pension program should "contain the best features of all the pension programs presently in operation by the four church bodies" and that it should be "put into operation immediately upon the formation of a new church or shortly thereafter." Furthermore, it should "be as uniform as possible with the least number of exceptions."

From this point on the actuarial and organizational details overwhelm the historian. He has before him a stack of reports and proposals measuring one solid inch, not counting a number of reports and the final texts of the constitutions and by-laws published in the Bulletin of Reports to the Detroit Convention. To report all that went on would be tediously lengthy—and even then inadequate. In a layman's, in this case a preacher's, summary it seems that a number of practical problems were faced by the committee and thereby the JCLU:

• What type of actuarial plan should be adopted?
• What should be the levels of payments and pensions?

- What was to be done about a lay pension plan?
- What was to be done about health benefits and death benefits?
- What was to be done about cases not previously covered by a plan similar to the one adopted?

Guided by the Committee on Pensions, the JCLU, meeting in September 1957, settled the first issue by passing a motion

> that the pension plan of the merged church shall be the money-purchase plan on an actuarial basis, with the pastor or other eligible persons and the congregations or organizations served by such contributing to the fund in which the member of the pension plan has an invested interest; with the understanding that money be made available from existing endowment funds and the budget of the general body to assure pensions of a reasonable size.

It is difficult to determine just when the payments levels were specified, but the Constitution of the Ministerial Pension and Death Benefit Plan, presented to and adopted by the constitutional convention in Detroit in 1962, specified in Articles III and IV that the pastor's contribution for a contributory member shall be 4 percent and that the contribution of the congregation shall be 8 percent. The evidence for competent work on lay pensions and health benefits is found in the Constitution of the Ministerial Health Benefit Plan and the Constitution of the Lay Pension Plan also presented to and adopted by the Detroit convention. The fifth issue, usually called hardship cases and mostly applicable to retired pastors of Suomi and the AELC who could not benefit from any contributory plan, or who could benefit very little, was discussed, and solemn promises were given orally that they would be cared for. Unfortunately, no one insisted that these promises be documented.

The main documentation of the planning done by the JCLU, mostly, of course, through a very competent committee that worked diligently and effectively over a period of five years, is found in the by-laws of the LCA:

LCA By-Laws, Section X, Boards, D. Board of Pensions.

Item 1. The Board of Pensions shall administer in behalf of this church such benefit plans as shall be adopted by the convention from time to time, including:

a. A contributory pension plan for ministers and missionaries, constructed on the money-purchase principle, in which the accumulated contributions attributed to each member's account are fully vested.

b. A supplemental non-contributory pension plan for ministers and missionaries ordained or commissioned prior to 1953.

c. Minimum pension and disability provisions for ministers and missionaries.

d. A plan yielding lump sum benefits to the survivors (1) of eligible members of the contributory pension plan, and (2) of certified theological students who have elected to participate therein.

e. A lay pension plan of the contributory type, for lay staff members and other lay employees of this church, its subsidiaries, institutions and congregations.

f. A plan providing medical, hospital and related benefits.

# 12. Conclusion

The task begun in December 1956 was coming to an end in May 1962. A great deal had been accomplished, commitments and decisions had been made, constitutions had been written, practical arrangements had been planned and executed. The argonauts had not brought back the golden fleece, but they delivered a cargo that they could view with satisfaction. There had been mistakes and failures along the way, of course. Not all hopes had been fulfilled, and certain issues were unsolved because differences could not be overcome. On the whole, however, the Commission members were satisfied. They had worked as a team with strong cooperation and fine understanding, and they had concentrated upon a given task with determination, competence, and efficacy. There had been little delay or whiling away of time. As a bellhop in a much-used hotel expressed it, "These Lutherans come with the Ten Commandments in the one hand and a ten-dollar bill in the other, and they don't break either."

The convention at Detroit was at hand, and it had been under preparation for months, first by a Committee for the Constituting Convention that had made all the necessary preparations from registration to the Communion service, second by committees that had prepared all the documents and instruments of adoption. Nominees had been selected for membership on boards, commissions, and agencies, and the nominations for top posts had been taken care of almost by common consent. Franklin Clark Fry was to be the president of the new church and Malvin H. Lundeen was to be the secretary. Only one item had become a cumbersome bottleneck that caused hard decisions and compromise maneuvers. This was the choice of top personnel for the boards.

The issue of selecting executive secretaries for the boards, the men who were to carry out the practical tasks of the new church, became a sensitive matter of confrontation. In one instance the two larger churches had strong candidates for a position and neither would give way. It would be easy to bypass this incident, but it would not be fair to the story of the JCLU to do so. This was the one issue, mentioned earlier, where delegations squared off in a roll-call vote. The confrontation was not one of the whole Commission, for there the votes were many and seldom disciplined. It took place in the Steering Committee, where each church had two votes, thus creating the possibility of a deadlock. In the matter of nomination for one board, four votes were thus cast for one candidate and four for another, two churches being aligned against two churches. For many ballots neither side would give way. Finally, the Steering Committee emerged with a compromise that settled the matter. The church whose candidate was not nominated gained the consideration that one of its prominent men was placed in a key position as secretary on another board, while the nominee for that board was shifted to a third board. There was some bitterness involved, but it was not a clash of the two large churches alone, for the two smaller churches also took sides. In the end there was a facing of reality. The goodwill of years of cooperation and the commitment to a common goal prevailed.

The Joint Commission on Lutheran Unity created the structure of a church. It did not create a church, for this is essentially the task of the spirit of God. The JCLU put together the framework of that supportive and consequential function of the worship fellowship which also, in our language, is called a church. It fashioned the structure to supply the needs of the worshiping fellowship according to the requirements of American society in the twentieth century. It tried to maintain that separation which is necessary in a free and pluralistic society in order to safeguard the essential treasures of the faith, but it tried also to maintain the spirit of brotherhood and cooperation that grows out of the gospel. It sought to be competent without being overburdened with organization, to be one without suppression of individual or regional values. It desired unity without imposed uniformity.

Evaluating the structure after fifteen years of function, it is apparent that its greatest and somewhat unforeseen impediment was bureaucracy on the one hand and the loss of that comfort and fellowship of individuals and congregations, which the Smalcald Articles call the "mutual conversation and consolation of the brethren," on the other. The two are related; fellowship fades in the face of regulations and regulatory agencies. The work of the Joint Commission should not be rejected or negated, however, by the fact that it could not foresee what life would be like a generation later. The Commission and its generation of leaders did their job; it is now the task to build a church life that will meet the needs of our time. That need is not structure but content, not hierarchy but humanity. If the structure-building did breed a generation of dominant domestics, thus fulfilling the Law of Parkinson, it is our task to fill the house with the freedom of life that is needed in our mechanistic society.

All in all, the "structuring of a church" was a competent and dedicated accomplishment, a monument to the hopes and dreams of mid-century America. It is better understood when its story is known, when we see what was accomplished and why. In a measure it satisfied the needs of men, and if it did not, it can be altered. Whether it found favor with the Lord of the church is not for men to judge. That this favor and the resultant guidance was sought in prayer and motivation, there can be no doubt, and the constant hope must be that the blessing of God's Holy Spirit was there. *Kyrie eleison!*

# Appendix: Commission and Committee Memberships

The following register of names is based in part on the documents of the JCLU and in part on a register included in Volume I of the bound minutes. The order of names is not alphabetical. It is given as found in the original documents. Titles are omitted.

It is an almost impossible and presumably fruitless task to list all the changes and substitutions that were made in the roster of commissioners and committee members, not to speak of substitutions at single sessions. To indicate some of the more important changes, the list of commissioners from March 1961 is added to the original roster.

ORIGINAL COMMISSIONERS—December 12, 1956

*American Evangelical Lutheran Church*

Alfred Jensen
H. O. Nielsen
Willard Garred
M. C. Miller
Ernest D. Nielsen
A. C. Kildegaard

Erik K. Moller
Johannes Knudsen
S. Dixon Sorenson
T. S. Hermansen
Martin Grobeck

*Augustana Evangelical Lutheran Church*

Oscar Benson
Wallace Anderson
Conrad Bergendoff
Lloyd L. Burke
Edgar M. Carlson
Thorsten A. Gustafson
Robert W. Holmen

Malvin H. Lundeen
Karl E. Mattson
D. Verner Swanson
P. O. Bersell
Lyman Brink
C. W. Sorensen

*Finnish Evangelical Lutheran Church of America*

Raymond W. Wargelin
Bernhard Hillila
Carl J. Tamminen
Douglas Ollila
A. Holmio

Walter Kukkonen
Karlo Keljo
Chester Heikkinen
Henry Kangas

*United Lutheran Church in America*

Franklin Clark Fry
Henry H. Bagger
Oscar W. Carlson
Charles M. Cooper
James F. Henninger
T. A. Kantonen
Frederick R. Knubel

Paul H. Krauss
Frank P. Madsen
Gilbert E. Olson
Howard Peterson
Dwight Putman
Carl C. Rasmussen

## COMMISSIONERS LISTED MARCH 1961

*AELC*

A. E. Farstrup
Willard Garred
Folmer Hansen
T. S. Hermansen
Alfred Jensen
A. C. Kildegaard

Johannes Knudsen
Harold H. Madsen
M. C. Miller
Erik K. Moller
Ernest D. Nielsen
H. O. Nielsen

*Augustana*

Malvin H. Lundeen
S. T. Anderson
Fred A. Carlson
Oscar A. Benson
Conrad Bergendoff
P. O. Bersell
Thorsten A. Gustafson

Robert Holmen
Leonard Kendall
Karl E. Mattson
Carl W. Segerhammer
C. W. Sorensen
D. Verner Swanson

*Suomi*

Raymond W. Wargelin
Bernhard Hillila
Armas Holmio
Ralph Jalkanen
Henry Kangas

Walter J. Kukkonen
Douglas Ollila
Eino Tuori
Alex Koski
Philip A. R. Anttila

*ULCA*

Franklin Clark Fry
Henry H. Bagger
Oscar W. Carlson
Charles M. Cooper
Voigt R. Cromer
George F. Harkins
T. A. Kantonen

Frank P. Madsen
Gilbert E. Olson
Howard Peterson
Carl C. Rasmussen
A. Howard Weeg
Dwight Putman

## OFFICERS

Malvin H. Lundeen, Chairman
Raymond W. Wargelin,
    Vice-Chairman

Carl C. Rasmussen, Secretary
Johannes Knudsen,
    Assistant Secretary and Treasurer

## STEERING COMMITTEE

Malvin H. Lundeen, Chairman
Carl C. Rasmussen, Secretary
Alfred Jensen
Oscar A. Benson
C. W. Sorensen
Raymond W. Wargelin

Franklin Clark Fry
James F. Henninger
A. E. Farstrup replaced
 Alfred Jensen
George Harkins replaced
 James Henninger

## COMMITTEE ON GEOGRAPHICAL BOUNDARIES

H. O. Nielsen, Chairman
T. A. Gustafson, Secretary

Raymond W. Wargelin
George Harkins

## COMMITTEE ON POWERS AND FUNCTIONS
### (at times called FUNCTIONS AND POWERS)

Bernhard Hillila, Chairman
Frank P. Madsen, Secretary
Alfred Jensen
Charles M. Cooper

Franklin Clark Fry
Oscar A. Benson
P. O. Bersell
D. Verner Swanson

## COMMITTEE ON DOCTRINE AND LIVING TRADITION

Karl E. Mattson, Chairman
Walter J. Kukkonen, Secretary

A. C. Kildegaard
T. A. Kantonen

## DRAFTING COMMITTEE

Malvin H. Lundeen, Chairman
Franklin Clark Fry
Raymond W. Wargelin

Alfred Jensen
Oscar A. Benson

## COMMITTEE ON POWERS AND FUNCTIONS OF OFFICERS
### AND AN EXECUTIVE BODY

C. W. Sorensen, Chairman
Ernest D. Nielsen, Secretary

Henry H. Bagger
Douglas Ollila

## COMMITTEE ON JUDICIARY

Chester Heikkinen, Chairman
Edgar M. Carlson

Henry Kangas
Dwight Putman

## COMMITTEE ON PENSIONS

O. V. Anderson, Chairman
George H. Berkheimer, Secretary
Armas Holmio
George W. Hansen

James F. Henninger
L. Edwin Wang, Consultant
Robert J. Myers, Consultant

## COMMITTEE ON PARISH EDUCATION

Walter B. Freed, Chairman
W. Kent Gilbert, Secretary
Howard Christensen
Frank Bonander
Marvin Raymond
Robert P. Hettico
Alfred L. Beck

L. Boyd Hamm
Martin J. Heinecken
Margaret J. Irvin
Harold U. Landis
Luther F. Schlenker
Lael Westberg, Consultant
S. White Rhyne, Consultant

## COMMITTEE ON FOREIGN MISSIONS

Ralph W. Loew, Chairman
Mrs. Ernest D. Nielsen, Secretary
Ralph Lindquist

J. Eugene Kunos
Malvin A. Hammarberg, Consultant
Earl S. Erb, Consultant

## COMMITTEE ON AMERICAN MISSIONS

Richard H. Sorensen, Chairman
Erwin List, Secretary
Thorsten A. Gustafson
Henry Kangas

T. E. Mattson, Consultant
R. H. Gerberding, Consultant
Donald L. Houser, Consultant

## COMMITTEE ON PUBLICATION HOUSE

Birger Swanson, Chairman
H. Torrey Walker, Secretary

Thorvald C. Hansen
Matt Laitala

## COMMITTEE ON CHURCH PAPERS

Joseph Sittler, Chairman
Thorvald Hansen, Secretary

O. V. Anderson
Ahti Karjala

## COMMITTEE ON PRINCIPLES OF ORGANIZATION, OBJECTS AND POWERS

Charles M. Cooper, Chairman
H. Conrad Hoyer, Secretary

David Halttunen
Johannes Knudsen

## COMMITTEE ON CONSTITUTIONS

Franklin Clark Fry, Chairman
James F. Henninger
P. O. Bersell

S. T. Anderson
Bernhard Hillila
Alfred Jensen

## LEGAL COMMITTEE

James F. Henninger, Chairman
Bernhard Levander
John W. Ansama

James W. Hall
Charles K. Woltz replaced
    James Henninger

## COMMITTEE ON SEMINARIES

P. O. Bersell, Chairman
Franklin Clark Fry

Ralph Jalkanen
Ronald Jespersen

## COMMITTEE ON COLLEGES

Erling Jensen, Chairman
Carl W. Segerhammer
David Halkala

A. Howard Weeg
Robert Mortved, Consultant

## COMMITTEE ON ELEEMOSYNARY INSTITUTIONS

Harold Haas, Chairman
Douglas Ollila

Holger P. Jorgensen
Lawrence Holt

## COMMITTEE ON BUDGET AND FINANCE

Martin E. Carlson, Chairman
Edmund F. Wagner
Otto K. Jensen

Floyd Anderson
M. C. Miller
Ray Piiparainen

## COMMITTEE ON HEADQUARTERS

A. Howard Weeg, Chairman
Leonard Kendall

Alfred Jensen
Raymond W. Wargelin

## COMMITTEE ON SEAL

Robert Hettico, Chairman
Wm. T. Schaeffer

W. R. Garred
Edgar S. Brown

## COMMITTEE ON CONSTITUTING CONVENTION

George F. Harkins, Chairman
Arthur E. M. Yeagy
N. Everett Hedeen

Thorsten A. Gustafson
A. E. Farstrup
V. A. Puotinen

## COMMITTEE ON NOMENCLATURE

Voigt R. Cromer, Chairman
Douglas Ollila

Carl W. Segerhammer
W. R. Garred

## COMMITTEE ON ARCHITECTURE

G. Martin Ruoss, Chairman
Harry Gjelsteen

Onni A. Koski
Reuben C. Anderson

## COMMITTEE ON WORSHIP

G. Everett Arden
A. C. Kildegaard

William R. Seaman

## COMMITTEE ON EVANGELISM

Alfred Stone, Chairman
Peter D. Thomsen
J. Sabin Swanson

Oliver Hallberg
William Berg, Consultant
J. Bruce Weaver, Consultant

## COMMITTEE ON STEWARDSHIP

Eugene S. Heckathron
Alfred L. Beck
LeRoy Breneman
Walter Hagey
Everett G. Mitchell
Clarence Stoughton
Everett Norling
Melville Sjostrand

Carl Hansen
Carl W. Segerhammer
Al Wellens
Rodney Davis
Earl Anderson
Harry C. Jensen
W. G. Ruohomaki

## COMMITTEE ON AUXILIARIES

Carl J. Tamminen
Oscar W. Carlson

Enok Mortensen
Leonard Kendall

## COMMITTEE ON MEN'S WORK

Sam Edwins
Clemens Zeidler

Enok Mortensen
Martin Saarinen

## COMMITTEE ON YOUTH WORK

Robert Hettico
David Gerberding
Donovan Palmquist

Howard Christensen
Richard Bringea
Raymond Tiemeyer

## JOINT COMMISSION ON LUTHERAN UNITY
## SUB-COMMITTEE ON WOMEN'S AUXILIARY

Mrs. Ernest Nielsen (AELC)
Miss Burnice Fjellman (Augustana)
Carl W. Segerhammer (Augustana)

Mrs. Ernest C. Pudas (Suomi)
Mrs. Charles W. Baker, Jr. (ULCA)
Howard Weeg (ULCA)

## JOINT PLANNING COMMITTEE—LUTHERAN CHURCH WOMEN

Mrs. Edwin E. Hansen (AELC)
Mrs. Johannes Knudsen (AELC)
Mrs. Ove R. Nielsen (AELC)
Mrs. Ralph Lindquist (Augustana)
Mrs. Carl W. Segerhammer
(Augustana)
Mrs. Bernard Spong (Augustana)
Miss Evelyn A. Stark, Consultant
(Augustana)

Mrs. Bert Mackey (Suomi)
Mrs. Mathias R. Ruohoniemi
(Suomi)
Mrs. Armas Wirtanen (Suomi)
Mrs. C. Gustav Bernstrom (ULCA)
Mrs. Ernest Tonsing (ULCA)
Mrs. Roy L. Winters (ULCA)
Miss Josephine Darmstaetter,
Consultant (ULCA)